SHRAVASTI
VIBRANT BUDDHIST HERITAGE

DR. K. P. WASNIK

BLUEROSE PUBLISHERS
India | U.K.

Copyright © K. P. Wasnik 2024

All rights reserved by author. No part of this publication may be reproduced, stored in a retrieval system or transmitted in any form or by any means, electronic, mechanical, photocopying, recording or otherwise, without the prior permission of the author. Although every precaution has been taken to verify the accuracy of the information contained herein, the publisher assumes no responsibility for any errors or omissions. No liability is assumed for damages that may result from the use of information contained within. Blue Rose Publishers takes no responsibility for any damages, losses, or liabilities that may arise from the use or misuse of the information, products, or services provided in this publication.

For permission requests or inquiries regarding this publication, please contact:

BLUEROSE PUBLISHERS,
NEW DELHI
www.BlueRoseONE.com
info@bluerosepublishers.com
+91 8882 898 898
+4407342408967

ISBN: 978-93-6452-702-6

Cover Design: Sadhna Kumari
Cover Picture Credit - Shri. Bhupendra Ganvir, Journalist, Writer from Nagpur
Conceptualization of cover page: Dr. K.P. Wasnik, Author
Typesetting: Pooja Sharma

First Edition: October 2024

THE BOOK IS DEDICATED TO

	Anathapindika invited Buddha to Shravasti and donated Jetavana (in 514-513 BCE) to Buddha and His Bhikkhu Sangha.
	Fa-Hien, the first Chinese Buddhist Monk who visited India (399 AD to 412 AD) and Shravasti and recorded what he had seen in Shravasti.
	Hsuan Tsang, the second Chinese Buddhist Monk who visited India and Shravasti (629 AD to 645 AD).He recorded what he had seen in Shravasti
	Sir Alexander Cunningham, a British Archaeologist, excavated Shravasti in 1863 AD and brought it to the world's attention.

FOREWORD

There is a plethora of ancient Buddhist heritage sites throughout the Indian subcontinent, from Bamiyan of Afghanistan to Angkor Wat of Cambodia, almost 6000 kms away from the mainland of India. Shravasti is one of those sites that remains vibrant and revered.

In his book 'Shravasti: A Vibrant Buddhist Heritage,' Dr. K. P. Wasnik carefully highlights the importance of this heritage in the life of the Buddha and Buddhism. Visiting this place even today, one would certainly feel the presence of the Exalted One, the Buddha, still lingering there. Dr. K. P.Wasnik has thus rightly documented the significance of Shravasti in his work and its pivotal role in the spread of the tenets of Buddhism among the people during the 6th Century BC through religious discourses. Today, this ancient heritage site is a major pilgrimage center for all Buddhists.

It was Sir Alexander Cunningham 1814 -1883 AD), the then Director General of the Archaeological Survey of India, who played a major role in unearthing Buddhist sites with Stupas, Monasteries all over the Indian Subcontinent.

After his enlightenment at Bodh Gaya, Lord Buddha traveled from place to place on foot for about 45 years to propagate the tenets of his new religion. It is noted that his first 'Varshavas' was conducted at Sarnath, and the last one, the 45th at Vaishali. Besides these two places, he held his Varshavas at Velugram Rajgir, Shravasti, Kapilvastu, Kushinagar, and other locations. According to Woodward, 871 suttas of the Buddhist canon were discussed by the Buddha during his stay at Shravasti. He also stated that the Buddha spent 25 Varshavas at Shravasti.

This work is not confined to the historical importance of Shravasti alone. The author goes beyond this to educate readers about the basic principles of Buddhism in a simple manner. He has presented

Shravasti and Buddhism in a straightforward manner that benefits ordinary men and women, helping them to lead a righteous life.

The author has rightly chosen this heritage site for his work, covering minute details about Shravasti and its significance in the Buddhist world, as it was the capital of the ancient Kosal kingdom. In writing about Shravasti, Dr. K. P.Wasnik has skillfully covered all the important places, their historical and religious significance, and the people associated with them, meticulously.Not only this, Dr. K.P.Wasnik has also documented the accounts of foreign travelers like Fa-Hien and Hiuen Tsang who traveled through India in the 4th and 7th centuries AD respectively to learn about Buddhism and to collect scriptures to be translated into Chinese for the benefit of their fellow countrymen.

Anathapindika donated the grove of Jetavan at Shravasti to the Buddha and the Sangha for their use during the rainy season. Today, most of the structural ruins from that period can be seen at the site of Jetavan, which were dedicated to the Buddha's most revered disciples.

I do not wish to intervene between the book and its readers for long. I am confident that this book will appeal to all. I take this opportunity to congratulate Dr. K. P. Wasnik for the laborious effort he has undertaken to bring out this book, which is presented in a simple and scrupulous manner. I wish Dr. Wasnik all the best.

- Vishwanath Shegaonkar. IAS (R)

Former Principal Secretary

The Govt of Tamil Nadu,Chennai

9840392005

vashegaonkar@gmail.com.

15th August, 2024

PREFACE

Shravasti holds deep historical and religious significance as the place where Gautama Buddha spent about 25 out of his 45 years of Dhamma life. Located in the modern-day Indian state of Uttar Pradesh, Shravasti was once the capital of the ancient Kingdom of Kosala, and now thrives as a major political, economic, and cultural center in Northern India. The city is revered in Buddhism as the primary site where many of the Buddha's teachings were delivered.

In Jainism, Shravasti is equally revered as the birthplace of the third Tirthankara, Sambhavanatha, with numerous temples and stupas reflecting its religious significance to Jains. Archaeological excavations have unearthed stupas, temples, monasteries, and ancient inscriptions, providing invaluable insights into Shravasti's rich historical and cultural heritage for Buddhists and Jains.

Notably, Shravasti is also mentioned in Buddhist literature as the capital of King Prasenjit, the Buddha's royal patron. In Shravasti, Anathapindaka, renowned for his philanthropy, purchased Jetavan Park and built residences for the Buddha and his Bhikkhus Sangha. Shravasti also witnessed many significant events, such as the conversion of Angulimala into a monk and the establishment of the Pubbarama Monastery by Vishakha.

Despite its profound significance, comprehensive books detailing Shravasti's past are notably scarce, leaving visitors and enthusiasts seeking more detailed information unsatisfied. Recognizing this gap, I embarked on writing a book to provide a thorough exploration of Shravasti's history and significance. The author endeavored to gather information from reports, historical documents, and archives, which also proved to be challenging due to the fragmented nature of existing sources. Nonetheless, the author aims to enrich readers' understanding and cater to the curiosity of tourists visiting this sacred site.

The author is immensely grateful to his family—his wife Jyotsna, daughters Aishwarya and Avantika, and his dear mother Smt. Pushpa—and his brothers Dayakar, Sunil, Ravindra, Naresh, and Chandrakant, for their unwavering support and encouragement throughout the writing process.

Special thanks are due to Shri Vishwanath Shegaonkar, IAS (Retd.), Former Principal Secretary to the Government of Tamil Nadu & writer whose insightful feedback and corrections have greatly enhanced the manuscript. I am also indebted to Shri Gulab Dhoke, Retired English Lecturer from Rajura, District Chandrapur, for his valuable contributions in improving the manuscript.

Additionally, I extend my gratitude to Dr. Anil Surya, a lyricist, writer, and poet from New Delhi; Shri Onkar Singh, General Manager at the National Seeds Corporation, New Delhi; Shri Jagdish Prasad, Section Officer in the Government of India; and Shri Sachin Ukey, IT Manager at the National Institute of Agricultural Marketing (NIAM), Jaipur.

Finally, I would like to thank the entire publication team of Blue Rose Publishers, New Delhi, for their meticulous efforts in publishing this book.

I invite you to share any additional information you may have about this city at kpwasnik2002@gmail.com. Your contributions will be invaluable for future editions of this book.

Dr. K. P. Wasnik

EG-12, Inderpuri,

New Delhi -12.

9891901316

kpwasnik2002@gmail.com.

31-8-2024

CONTENTS

1. SHRAVASTI 1
2. HISTORICAL IMPORTANCE OF SHRAVASTI 4
   - Sahet Mahet is Shravasti
   - Shravasti in Jain Literature
   - Buddha spent 25 rainy seasons in Shravasti
   - Descriptions of Shravasti by Chinease Travellers
   - Excavation of Jetavana by Brtitishers
   - Fall of Shravasti
3. PEOPLE ASSOCIATED WITH SHRAVASTI 21
   - Anathapindika
   - Angulimala
   - Queen Mallika
   - King Prasenjit
   - Vishaka
4. IMPORTANT EVENTS IN SHRAVASTI 56
   - Untouchable Sunit became Monk
   - Two important decisions in Shravasti
   - Allegations of Muder against Buddha and Sangha
   - Buddha was falsely accused of sexual misconduct.
   - Sad story of Bhikkhuni Patachara
   - Utpalvarna became Bhikkhuni
   - Story of Kisa Gautami
   - Death of Devadatta in Jetavana
5. DHAMMA SERMONS GIVEN BY BUDDHA IN
SHRAVASTI 81
   - To the General Public

- Address to King Prasenjit
- To Anathapindika
- To Vishaka
- To Bhikkhu Sangha

6. IMPORTANT TOURIST PLACES IN SHRAVASTI 202
- Jetavana Monastry
- Orajhar
- Purvarama Mahavihara
- Anathapindika's Stupa - Kachi Kuti
- Angulimala Stupa - Pakki Kuti
- Ghantaghar
- Vipassana Dhyan Kendra
- Mynmar and Korean Temple
- Shobhanath Temple

7. HOW TO REACH SHRAVASTI 222
- By Road
- By Air
- By Rail
- Accomodation in Shravasti
- The best time to visit Shravasti
- Other important information
- Why to visit Shravasti

8. BIBLIOGRAPHY 226

1. SHRAVASTI

Shravasti is a city in the Indian state of Uttar Pradesh. It was the capital of the ancient Indian kingdom of Kosal Kingdom, where the Buddha spent about 25 rainy seasons after his enlightenment. Shravasti is situated at a distance of just 40 kilometers from Bahraich, a district near the India-Nepal border, located at the foothills of the Himalayas. It is surrounded by the districts of Balrampur and Bahraich in Uttar Pradesh and by Nepal. Shravasti was carved out from the districts of Gonda and Bahraich. Bhinga town serves as district headquarters of Shravasti, which falls under the Devipatan Revenue Division.

Shravasti is situated on the banks of the Rapti River, and the main language spoken here is Hindi. Shravasti district was officially formed on May 22, 1997. However, its existence was abolished by the government on January 13, 2004. The district was reestablished in June 2004. The district headquarters of Shravasti is 175 kilometers away from the state capital, Lucknow. The area of the district is 2,458 square kilometers, which consists of 3 tehsils and 5 blocks, namely Ikauna, Hariharpurrani, Gilola, Jamunha, and Sirsia, and 536 inhabited villages. The estimated population in 2022 is 13,05,062 and the district is predominantly rural, with agriculture being the mainstay of livelihood.

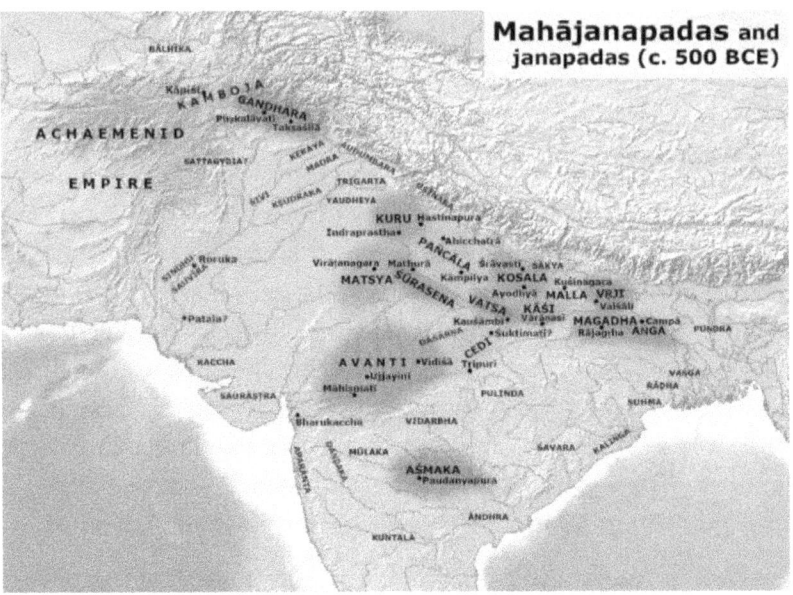

Its population growth rate in the decade 2001–2011 stood at 30.54%. The sex ratio in Shravasti district was 881 females per 1,000 males. The male literacy rate was 57.16%, while the female literacy rate was 34.78%. This district has a strong rural base, with more than 96 % of the population living in rural areas. Scheduled Castes and Scheduled Tribes constitute 16.94% and 0.50% of the population, respectively. Though the district is Hindu-dominated, it has a large number of Muslims. Although it was formerly a center of Buddhism, currently fewer than a thousand Buddhists live in the district.

According to the 2011 Census of India, 87.55% of the population in the district spoke Hindi, 11.17% Awadhi, and 1.15% Urdu as their first language. The local dialect is Awadhi. Shravasti is an important place for tourism. It is a small town, but it serves as a center of heritage tourism and religious pilgrimage for Buddhists from all over the world. This district of Uttar Pradesh is recognized as a Buddhist pilgrimage site from all over the world. Besides the heritage sites like Jetavana, Pubbarama, Angulimala Kuti, several countries like Sri Lanka, Myanmar, Thailand, China, and South Korea - have built their own monasteries. A meditation center, built by Thailand, attracts a large number of foreign tourists.

Shravasti is also a place of worship for followers of the Hindu religion. There are well-known temples in the area, such as Vibhuti Nath and

Sonpathari. Lakhs of people come to Vibhuti Nath on the occasion of Kajari Teej fair. Sambhavnath, the third Tirthankar of Jainism, was born here and made this place his seat for the spread of Jainism. The 8th and 24th Tirthankaras of the Jain religion also visited this place. It is said that Mahavira, the 24th and last Tirthankara, visited Shravasti several times. There are accounts of his great debates on Dharma with Makkhali Gosala (560–484 BCE), the founder of the Ajivika sect.

Shravasti has several educational institutions, including Chaudhary Ram Bihari School, Buddha Inter College, Janta Inter College, and Subhash Inter College in Ikauna, which provide quality education to many students. However, in other areas of development, Shravasti has inadequate infrastructure in health, nutrition, rural education, agriculture, economic development, employment, infrastructure, transport, and communication. Shravasti is listed as one of the backward districts in the state by the Central Government, due to its low development index. It is the least literate district among all the 75 districts of Uttar Pradesh. Despite the fertile land, the district remains poverty-stricken. Additionally, almost every year there is a loss of life and property due to floods in the Rapti River. Flooding is a recurring problem in the district, with flash floods originating from the rivers of neighboring Nepal. The situation is further exacerbated by the prevailing unemployment, migration, and lack of industries in the district.

Despite gaining international recognition as an important Buddhist destination, Shravasti still lacks a well-equipped bus station. Even after 20 years since the formation of the district, the people here continue to face challenges due to inadequate transportation facilities. Every year, lakhs of devotees and tourists from all over the world arrive here, but due to a lack of transport facilities, they are forced to rely on private modes of transport. Shravasti suffers from inadequate transportation infrastructure, poor road conditions, and limited connectivity, which hinders economic activities.

Despite its historical and religious significance, the district has not been able to leverage its historical and cultural heritage for effective economic and tourism development.

2. HISTORICAL IMPORTANCE OF SHRAVASTI

Sahet-Mahet is Shravasti

Shravasti is one of the most revered sites for Buddhism. It was here that Buddha delivered many of his Dhamma Suttas (sermons) to many of his disciples.The remains of Shravasti, the capital of the Kosal kingdom of ancient India is the modern places called 'Sahet- Mahet'. Sahet-Mahet village, now 12 miles west of Balrampur.

More recently, a century ago, Vincent Arthur Smith CIE (3 June 1843 – 6 February 1920) was an Irish Indologist, historian, member of the Indian Civil Service and curator, first argued that ancient Shravasti to be the present-day Sahet Mahet. This was corroborated by the findings of Shri. Govind Chand Gahadwal's discovery of an inscription of 1128 AD from the excavation of Jetavana, which had confirmed its equation with 'Sahet-Mahet'. Mahet is the place of ancient Shravasti and Sahet is the place of a Buddhist monastery, i.e. a Jetavana.

According to the Buddhist texts, a sage named Avath Shravasta lived here, and the city was named after him as Shravasti. According to the Epics, Puranas, and other scriptures, Shravasti was named after Shravast or Shravastak, who was the son of Yuvanay and was born in the sixth generation of Prithu. He was the creator of this city, and hence, it was named Shravasti after him.

According to another legend, this city was named Shravasti after the Suryavanshi King Shravasta. It is said that the legendary King Shravasta founded this city. Shravasti was the capital of the Kosal Empire for about 1000 years, from the 6th century BC to the 6th century AD.

According to Buddhist scriptures, all the small and big things needed in daily life were easily available in abundance in this prosperous city. Hence, it was called Savatthi (सब्ब अट्ठी).

Shravasti was considered one of the six metropolitan cities of India during the Buddha's time. Those cities were Champa, Rajgruha, Shravasti, Saket, Kosambi, and Varanasi. During the lifetime of the Lord Buddha, Shravasti was the capital of Kosal country and was a prosperous and commercially important trading place in those days. As a capital, Shravasti was at the junction of three major trade routes in ancient India that connected it with various regions of the Indian subcontinent. This prosperous trading center was famous for its religious associations. The material prosperity of Shravasti was at its peak during the reign of King Ashoka the Great. King Ashoka also is credited with the construction of two 21-meter-high pillars, as well as several monasteries and stupas in and around Shravasti.

The ancient city of Shravasti was situated on the banks of the Achiravati river, whose modern name is Rapti. In the Buddhist era, this river used to flow close to the city, encircling the whole populace.

Shravasti in Jain Literature

Shravasti is often mentioned in Jain literature too and it is also called Chandrapuri or Chandrikapuri. According to the Jain texts, it is said that two Tirthankaras–Sambhavanath(3rd of 24 Tirthankaras) and Chandraprabhanatha (8th of 24 Tirthankaras) were born there. The 'Shobhanatha' temple is considered to be the birthplace of Jain Tirthankara 'Sambhavanath', which has made Shravasti an important center for Jains. As mentioned in the 'Brihatkalpa' and various Kalpas of the 14th century, the name of the city was Mahet. Shravasti is the holy place where the conception, birth, penance, and Kevaljnana welfare of Lord Sambhavanath, the third Tirthankara, were celebrated. Furthermore, Shravasti is the place of bitter arguments and debates between the 24th Tirthankara Mahavira and Makkhali Gosala, the founder of the Ajivikas Sect. According to Jain texts, Mahavira visited Shravasti several times and spent some rainy seasons here. Ancient Jain scholars like Kapila, Maghavan, and Keshi studied at Shravasti. In ancient times, Shravasti was a very famous Jain pilgrimage site.

Over time, many temples, stupas, viharas, and pillars were built here. The ancient temple of Lord Sambhavanath is currently in a dilapidated condition. It is now called the Shobhanath Temple. It is believed that there may be 18 more temples around the Shobhanath temple, one of which could be the birthplace of Lord Chandraprabhanatha, the 8th Tirthankara. The first temple was consecrated in 1966 by organizing the Panch Kalyanak Pratishtha Mahotsav. In this temple, a 3 feet and 9 inches high white attractive idol of Lord Sambhavanath is in a sitting posture and was installed as the main deity. This idol is miraculous and charming. The consecration of the second temple took place in the year 1995. It is extremely beautiful, attractive, and equipped with high artistic features. The idols of 24 Tirthankaras along with the main deity Lord Sambhavanath are installed in this temple. This 84-foot-high temple is called the Lord Sambhavnath Chaubisi Temple. Shravasti was ruled by Jain kings from 900 AD to 1000 AD. In year 900 A.D. Jain king Mayudhwaj, in 925 A.D. Jain King Hansdhwaj, in 950 A.D. Jain King Makradhwaj, in 975 A.D. Jain King Sudhandwadhwaj and in 1000A.D. Jain King Suhurddhwaj ruled here.

Buddha spent 25 rainy seasons in Shravasti.

This is the same area where Gautama Buddha spent about 25 of his 45 years of Dhamma life in Shravasti. Shravasti is the principal site where almost all of the Buddha's teachings were either heard or compiled, and recorded elsewhere centuries later as the Pali Canon. According to Woodward, almost 871 suttas from the four Nikayas of Buddhism were preached at Shravasti. Of these suttas, about 844 were preached in the monastery of Jetavana, 27 were preached in the monastery of Pubbarama, and the remaining 4 were preached in the suburbs of Shravasti. Thus, Shravasti became the place where the greatest number of suttas were delivered by the Lord Buddha.

Shravasti is also mentioned as the capital of Buddha's royal patron, King Prasenjit. It was also the home of Anathapindika, the richest donor of the Buddha. Anathapindika is famous in Buddhist literature as the one who offered the Jetavana garden to Buddha and his Sangha. Angulimala, a notorious dacoit who looted travelers in the forest, cut off their fingers and wore them as a garland, was accepted by Buddha as his follower at this very place on the banks of the Rapti River. Even today, there is the Bodhi tree at this place where Gautam Buddha used to sit and preach Dhamma to his followers. Buddhist lady Vishakha, the daughter-in-law of Shravasti's banker Migara, had built a new monastery, Purvaram (Pubbaram), to the northeast of Jetavana. During the time of Buddha, there were two monasteries named Jetavana and Purvarama (Pubbarama). Pubbarama was also known as Pubbarama Migara Mata Pasada and had a two-story building with five hundred rooms on the ground floor and the same number on the upper floor. In this city, Ashoka the Great and his grandson King Samprati built many temples, monasteries, stupas, etc.

The site was abandoned and fell into ruins by the end of the Gupta period in the 5th century AD. In addition, the ruins of many stupas and 'Sahet-Mahet' are visible today. The remains of ruined buildings in the Jetavana area of Shravasti remain centers of faith, where Buddhist followers from around the world come to this pilgrimage site with devotion and consider themselves blessed. The Chakravarti king Ashoka, the great visited Shravasti in 249 BCE as a part of his pilgrimage to this sacred Buddhist site who had ordered the installation of two 70 feet high pillars along with the relics of the Buddha on either side of the eastern gate of Jetavana. Additionally, some stupas were also built. The western part of Mahet is rich in remains of Jain architecture and art, including temples, monasteries, stupas, sculptures, and other structures dating back to the 4th century BCE. Over time, forests had naturally grown over the remains of Shravasti and its surrounding areas.

Description of Shravasti by Chinese Travellers

1. Fa-Hien

Fa-Hien was a Chinese Buddhist monk and translator who walked from China to India to obtain Buddhist literature. Fa-Hien is also known as Fa-hsien, Sehi and Faxian who was born in 337 AD in Pingyang Wuyang, modern Linfen City, Shanxi. His original family name was Gong, and his birth name was Sehi. Fa-Hien was orphaned at a young age and spent most of his adult life in Buddhist monasteries. He later adopted the name Faxian, which literally means 'Splendor of the Dharma'. Three of his elder brothers died young. His father, worried that he would meet the same fate, therefore, he had been ordained as a novice monk at the age of three.

In 399 AD, he began his grueling trip with 4 others at the age of 62 to the Land of the Buddha to discover Buddhist texts. He traveled between 399AD and 412 AD across India. The biggest feature of his journey to India was that he traveled on foot from China to India. Faxian had the distinction of being the first Chinese traveler to travel to India, setting out an expedition through Central Asia to India and eventually to Sri Lanka.

*This image shows the route taken by **Fa Hien** as he traveled from China to India.*

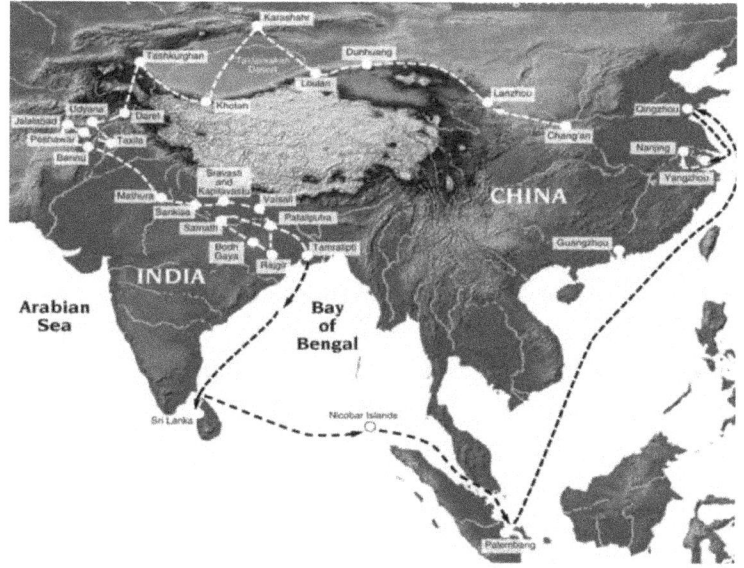

Faxian's journey: Map illustration by Willa Davis

He arrived in Patliputra from the northwest, which was under the reign of Chandragupta II. From his visit to Patliputra, Fa-Hien reasoned that there were various Sanghas of both the Hinayana and Mahayana sects that educated students from across India. In a Buddhist monastery, he uncovered a copy of the Vinaya Pitaka, which includes the Mahasanghika laws written in Sanskrit. Therefore, he stayed in Pataliputra for about three years, learned Sanskrit, and wrote the Vinaya Niyamas or rules.

He stayed in India for almost 10 years, the longest time he spent in any country. He traveled to many cities and wrote about Peshawar, Kannauj and places associated with the life of Buddha – Bodhgaya, Lumbini, Kapilvastu, Shravasti, Sarnath, Vaishali, Rajgir, Taxila, Pataliputra, Mathura, Shravasti and Kannauj and other places in India.

Political and Administrative Recordings

Fa-Hien visited India during the reign of Chandragupta II on a religious mission. Chandragupta II (375-415AD), also known by his title Vikramaditya, as well as Chandragupta Vikramaditya. He was the third ruler of the Gupta Empire in India. Chandragupta II is regarded as one of the greatest rulers of the Gupta dynasty. Chandragupta II was the son of Samudragupta and Datta Devi. According to historical records, Chandragupta II was a strong, vigorous ruler who was well qualified to govern and expand the Gupta Empire.

Fa-Hien wrote about Chandragupta II that he was a very kind and generous king who worked for the welfare of his people. Chandragupta II ran several charitable institutions, free health services, and rest houses for traders and travelers. Public morality was very high during the reign of Chandragupta II. People respected each other's beliefs, traditions, and customs. Chandragupta II gave great emphasis and importance to Pataliputra (modern Patna). Therefore, it was a beautiful, orderly and clean city with many wealthy people. People were prosperous, cheerful, liberal and morally strong. They were generally vegetarians, abstaining from intoxicants such as wine and other narcotics. There were residences set up to provide charity and medicine as well as massive donations made to temples, monasteries, and sanghas, among other things. People were content with their lifestyles. The monarchs and affluent individuals built rest-houses that provided travelers with every convenience. Hospitals were also built for low-income groups with free drugs. According to Fa Hien's account, the Gupta period was humane and prosperous with peace, morality, and security across the empire.

He was impressed by Ashoka's palace at Pataliputra, which was in existence even during the Gupta era. Fa-Hien argued that the palace was so beautiful, therefore that must have been erected not by mankind but by the gods. He also mentioned the remains of a stupa and two monasteries nearby, both of which were attributed to Ashoka. He also took notice of Emperor Ashoka's inscriptions, the Lion Capital and the Sanchi Stupa.

Fa-Hien also visited Malwa, where he was affected by the scorching climate. He said that India's internal and external trade was growing, and that Indians were increasingly taking part in maritime trade. According to Fa-Hien, India had ports such as Cambay, Sopara and Baroach on the Western sea coast, while Tamralipti was a well-known port on the Eastern sea coast. Fa-Hien embarked on an Indian ship while traveling to Sri Lanka from this port.

Religious Recordings

According to Fa-Hien's records, Buddhism and Hinduism coexisted at that time, and people exhibited religious tolerance. Buddhism was becoming more popular in Punjab, Bengal, and Mathura. Hinduism was increasingly widespread as the Gupta kings primarily patronized Hindu social orders. During Chandragupta II's reign, the Gupta Empire expanded across areas such as Uttar Pradesh, Bihar and a portion of Bengal.

Fa-Hien's account provides valuable details about his experiences visiting Indian states and the status of Buddha and its teachings in India and beyond. Fa-Hien's detailed descriptions and recordings provide insight into the life and teachings of Gautama Buddha, the traditions, philosophy and principles of Buddhism, as well as information about the kings, society and their governance.

What did Fa-Hien document about Shravasti?

According to Fa-Hien, Buddhism was thriving in North-Western India, though it was declining in the Ganges valley. In his document, Fa-Hien mentioned the unsatisfactory condition of some Buddhist holy places he visited. During his visit to Shravasti in 407 AD, Fa-Hien wrote that the seven-story main building of the Jetavana monastery was accidentally destroyed by fire. Pubbarama, built by Vishakha, was also completely ruined. The extensive garden of Jetavana Vihara had two gates, one opening towards the East and the other towards the North. To the North- East of Jetavanaa was a stupa where the Buddha cleansed a sick monk with water. There was another vihara in which a huge statue of about 60 feet of the Lord Buddha was installed.

His visit to Sri Lanka

In 411 AD, Fa-Hien travelled to Ceylon (modern Sri Lanka) from the port of Tamralipati (in modern West Bengal). Fa-Hien spent two years in Sri Lanka and decided to return to China by an uncertain sea route. Fa-Hien is currently memorialized by a cave in the Kalutara district of Sri Lanka. It is believed that he lived there.

His Autobiography

He took a huge quantity of Sanskrit writings with him, whose translations inspired East Asian Buddhism and served as a prologue for numerous historical figures, events, texts, and ideas. When he returned home at the age of 77 years, he translated the Buddhist sutras. He wrote a travelogue with crucial details of his travel experiences in India, covering the public life, the state of Buddhism and places related to his Dhamma. His travelogue is called Fo-Kwo-Ki (A Record of Buddhist Kingdoms; also known as Faxian's Account). His autobiography is a valuable independent account of early Buddhist practices in India. In Jingzhou, China, Faxian died at the age of 88 years. His autobiography is an unbiased account of early Buddhism in India. In simple words, his recordings are still a valuable source of information for Indian history.

2. Hiuen Tsang (Xuanzang)

Hiuen Tsang, a Chinese Buddhist monk, came to India during the reign of King Harshavardhana from 629 to 645 AD. He visited many places related to Buddhism in India for 15 years. Hiuen Tsang (602 AD – 664 AD) was a 7th-century Chinese Buddhist monk, scholar, traveler, and translator. Hiuen Tsang was born on 6 April 602 AD in Chenliu, now Henan Province in China. His family was renowned for its scholarship for generations and Hiuen Tsang was the youngest of four children. His ancestor was Chen Xi, a Minister of the Eastern Han dynasty. His grandfather Chen Cong was a Professor at the Taixue Academy (Imperial Academy). His father Chen Hui served as a Magistrate of Jiangling County during the Sui dynasty. According to traditional biographies, Hiuen Tsang displayed brilliant intelligence and honesty while studying with his father. As a boy, he began reading religious books with his father and studied various ideas contained in them.

His elder brother was already a monk in a Buddhist monastery. He also got inspired at a young age. Hiuen Tsang expressed interest in becoming a Buddhist monk like his brother. After his father's death in 611 AD, he lived for five years at Jingtu Monastery with his elder brother Chen Su. During this time, he studied Mahayana Sect as well as various early Buddhist schools.

Hiuen Tsang was ordained as a Shramanera (novice monk) at the age of thirteen. Due to the political and social unrest caused by the fall of the Sui dynasty, he moved to Chengdu, Sichuan, where he was ordained as a monk at the age of twenty. He came to Changan, which was then under the peaceful rule of Emperor Taizong of Tang, where Hiuen Tsang developed a desire to visit India. He was aware of Fa-Hien's visit to India, and like him, he was concerned about the incomplete and misinterpreted Buddhist texts recorded in China. He was also concerned about completing Buddhist doctrines in the diverse Chinese translations.

At the age of 27, he began his long journey towards India. He violated his country's ban on foreign travel and reached India via Central Asian cities. He reached the city of Hami from the Gobi Desert. He crossed Central Asia, covering Kyrgyzstan, Tashkent, Samarkand in Uzbekistan. He also crossed the Pamir Mountains, Hind Kush. Next, he reached the Amu, Darya river in Central Asia and Afghanistan, and Termez, where he encountered over a thousand Buddhist monks. On reaching Afghanistan, he saw various Buddhist sites which were almost ruined. In Afghanistan, he met the monk Dharmasimha and more than 3,000 non-Mahayana monks. He had also acquired the important texts of Mahavibhasha, which he later translated into Chinese. Hiuen Tsang arrived in central Afghanistan and visited dozens of non-Mahayana monasteries and saw a Buddha statue carved out of hard rock at Bamiyan. Resuming the journey, he reached Kabul and saw more than 100 Mahayana monasteries and 6000 monks in various monasteries.

In 630 AD, Hiuen Tsang reached the ancient land of Gandhara. On leaving Adinapura (now Jalalabad in Afghanistan), he visited various stupas and then crossed the Khyber Pass to reach Purushapura (now Peshawar in Pakistan), the capital of Gandhara. Here, he saw the Kanishka Stupa. Crossing the Swat valley, he reached Udayan, where he saw monasteries housing 18,000 monks. Moving towards the Berner valley and Shahbaz Garhi, he crossed the Indus River to reach Taxila. In Takshashila, Hiuen Tsang found that most of the Sangharams (temples and monasteries) were in a ruined and in desolate condition due to prevailing infighting between the local rulers.

Xuanzang reached Kashmir in 631 AD where he found more than 100 monasteries and about 5,000 monks in the region spreading the message of the Lord Buddha.

Hiuen Tsang reached Matipura (today known as Mandawar near Bijnor in Uttar Pradesh) in 634 AD. At the Matipura Monastery, Hiuen Tsang studied under the Buddhist monk Mitrasena. The places he visited in India included Jalandhar in Punjab, Kullu in Himachal Pradesh, Bairat in Rajasthan, Mathura in Uttar Pradesh, and a few other locations associated with the life of the Buddha. During those times, Mathura, although a Hindu-majority place, had 2,000 monks from major Buddhist branches.

Xuanzang crossed the Yamuna and Ganga rivers to reach Kannauj, the grand capital of the North Indian empire of King Harsha Vardhana. In Kannauj, he saw 100 monasteries with 10,000 monks, and was impressed by King Harsha's patronage of both scholarship and the promotion of Buddhism. He spent time studying early Buddhist scriptures in the city. In 636 AD, he visited Givishan (Kashipur), Ayodhya (the homeland of the Yogakara School), and Kaushambi. After this, he returned to Shravasti in Uttar Pradesh and then he went to Terai in Nepal. In 637 AD, Hiuen Tsang started his voyage from Lumbini towards Kushinagar, Sarnath, Varanasi, Vaishali, Patna, and Bodhgaya. He also visited the Champa Math in Bhagalpur.

He spent approximately five years at the renowned Nalanda University in the state of Bihar. There, he studied logic, grammar, Sanskrit and the Yogacara school of Buddhism. At Nalanda, he met the Venerable Silbhadra, an expert in Yogachara teachings who was also his personal teacher. While studying Buddhism at Nalanda University, Hiuen Tsang discovered ten commentaries on Vasubandhu. From Nalanda, Hiuen Tsang traveled to Bangladesh, where he discovered 20 monasteries and more than 3,000 monks studying Buddhism. At the invitation of the Assamese king Kumar Bhaskara Varman, Hiuen Tsang went to the ancient city of Prag Jyotishpura in the state of Kamrup (now Guwahati) in the East.

He also visited Samatata, Tamralipti, Kalinga, and other regions in the East, which he named '*The Domain of Eastern India*'.

He then travelled to Andhra Pradesh and visited the viharas at Amravati and Nagarjunakonda. In Amravati, he studied the texts of Abhidhamma Pitaka. He continued his journey to Kanchi, the royal capital of the Pallavas and a strong center of Buddhism in South India. Before returning to Nalanda, he visited Nasik, Ajanta Caves, Malwa, Multan, and the Pravata region.

At the request of King Harshavardhana, Hiuen Tsang was brought back to Kannauj to attend a great Buddhist gathering. The gathering was attended by neighboring kings, Buddhist monks, Brahmins, and

Jains. King Harsha also invited Hiuen Tsang to the Kumbh Mela at Prayag, where he witnessed King Harsha generously distributing gifts to the poor. Then, he was given a grand farewell by the king.

What he saw in Shravasti during his journey

When he visited Shravasti in 637 AD, he wrote in his travel diary that the capital Shravasti was in a state of ruins with a few inhabitants, without defining its territories. There were definitely some temples at that time, in which a few monks were residing. Ancient monasteries, temples, pillars etc. all had started getting destroyed. Only the city walls remained and vegetation had grown on most of the buildings. Only a settlement of about 200 families had remained there.

Efforts were being made to build new monasteries and temples in their respective places. Only the foundation of Prasenjit's palace remained intact. To the east, he saw the Great Dhamma Hall Stupa, another stupa, and the temple of Buddha's maternal aunt Mahaprajpati Gautami. Beyond these, he saw the great stupa of Angulimala. There were good crops in that area and the weather was also good. The people's way of earning was honest and they were interested in good deeds. To the northwest of the capital Shravasti, he saw a series of stupas built by King Ashoka, the Great.

His Travelogue

Traveling through the Khyber Pass, Hind Kush, Kashgar, Khotan, Hiuen Tsang returned to China. It took him 16 years to return to China, and he arrived there in 645 AD. After returning to China, he retired to a monastery and devoted his life to writing travelogues and studying Buddhist philosophy. This Chinese travelogue, titled *'Great Tang Records on the Western Regions'* is a notable source about Hiuen Tsang. His travelogue is a mixture of legends, hearsay, and firsthand observations from his time in India.

He is known for his landmark contributions to Chinese Buddhism, his travelogue of his journey to India from 629–645 AD, and his efforts to carry over 657 Indian texts to China on the backs of yaks.

Excavation of Jetavana by the Britishers

Many old religious and historical ancient sites were excavated by the Britishers during their rule over India. Many Buddhist sites were abandoned for various reasons, and over time, these sites turned into forests and dunes. The person who played a major role in the discovery of Buddhist sites across India was Sir Alexander Cunningham (1814-1893 AD) who was the Director General (from 1st January 1871) of the Department of Archaeological Survey of India and often regarded as the father of Indian Archaeology.

MAJOR-GENERAL SIR ALEXANDER C. CUNNINGHAM, K.C.S.I., C.I.E.,
LATE BENGAL ENGINEERS.

A military disciplinarian, he was involved in archaeology when he excavated at Sārnāth, near Vārānasi (Benares). In 1850, he excavated Sānchi, site of some of the oldest surviving buildings in India. In addition to a study of the temple architecture of Kashmir in 1848 and a work on Ladakh in 1854, he published *The Bhilsa Topes* (1854), the first serious attempt to trace Buddhist history through its architectural remains. He had a natural concern for ancient remains and was deeply troubled by the way monuments were destroyed through vandalism and the destruction of nature. When Sir Alexander Cunningham was appointed Surveyor of the Archaeological Survey of India in 1861, he led the survey of North India by adopting the travel records of the famous Chinese Buddhist monks Fa-Hien and Hiuen Tsang. Their travelogues proved to be very helpful to him in locating many ancient Buddhist sites like Lumbini, Kapilvastu, Kushinara, Sankasiya, Nalanda, Kosambi, Shravasti and many other places which had been lost over time.

The first attempt to bring to light the ancient glory of Shravasti in modern times was made by Sir Alexander Cunningham. He started the excavation of the ruins of Shravasti in 1862 AD. In about a year's work, he cleared part of Jetavana, and in 1863, Sir Cunningham identified the twin ruins of huge mounds called Sahet and Mahet. He excavated ruins spread over an area of 13 hectares at Sahet and identified them as Jetavana. He recovered a 7 feet 4 inches high statue of Buddha. This was the same idol that had been installed by Bhikshu Bal. The most important of these items was an inscribed copper plate, which was a donation letter from the King Govind Chandra of Kannauj. The ruins of Mahet were spread over 162 hectares.

Based on these inscriptions, scholars have concluded that Sahet was the area of Jetavana, and Mahet was the area of Shravasti. In 1876 AD, General Conningham re-excavated these places and he discovered sixteen different buildings, mostly stupas and small temples. He uncovered the ruined structures of several stupas, viharas, and monasteries, including the Gandhakuti (fragrant chamber) and the Kosambi Kuti. According to him, a huge statue of Bodhisattva was also found, and that monastery was called Kosamba Kuti. To its north was Gandhakuti, the main temple. The ruins include platforms and foundations of various monastic establishments, and some stupas were in a more or less well-preserved state. The colossal Buddhisattva statue and some other fragments discovered by Cunningham were Buddhist sculptures belonging to the Kushan period and were carved in Mathura. The huge, headless statue of Buddha at Shravasti was similar to the statues of Buddha at Sarnath, Mathura, and Allahabad, which were donated by Bhikkhu Bala, and crafted by the same sculptor. The ruins of the royal palace or any residential house had not yet been discovered.

Dr. W. Hoey began a very intensive search from 15th December 1884 to 15th May 1885. One of the important discoveries made by Dr. Hoey was a well-preserved stone inscription dated 1119 AD. The monuments found during the excavations were identified as described by Fa-hien and Hiuen Tsang in their travelogues. In 1885, Dr. W. Hoey brought to light some more monuments in the area of Mahet. He recovered some sculptures from the ruins of the Jain temple Shobhanath, located west of Mahet.

Twenty-three years later, on 3 February 1908, Dr.J.P.H.Vogel started excavation at this site with the assistance of Rai Bahadur alias Dayaram Sahni. Among the statues found at the site were those related to the Buddha. In 1910-11AD, under the chairmanship of renowned archaeology expert Sir John Marshal, Dr. Bogle along with Shri Dayaram Sahini excavated the ruins of this area for about three months and brought many important objects to light. Among these, there was an inscribed footstool of the Buddha statue, on which Jetavana was mentioned. Most of the sculptures found in Shravasti and Jetavana were related to Buddhism. Some clay idols, toys, and other artifacts were also unearthed from Kachhi Kuti which had artistic and historical importance. Many monasteries, stupas, Bodhisattva statues, coins, clay statues, and seals were also unearthed in the area of Sahet. The discovery of numerous charcoal remains and burnt soil suggests that a large part of the sites was burnt and damaged, while other parts became unusable due to decay and erosion.

Fall of Shravasti

Sir Alexander Cunnigham in his book '*Bhilsa Topes* (1854)' briefed historical sketch of the rise, progress and decline of Buddhism in India. He mentioned in his book that in India, from the fifth to seventh century AD, the decline of Buddhism was gradual and gentle. But the further progress of decay was then stayed for a time. In the seventh century, Buddhism was propagated throughout Tibet and adjoining countries. The magnificent stupa at Sarnath, which stands two hundred feet in height was erected and a colossal copper image of Buddha was set up, and several chaityas and viharas were built by the great Lalitaditya in Kashmir. However, from the 18th century onward, the decline of Buddhism was rapid and violent. The new dynasties that arose did not prioritize Buddhism, as they were influenced by the Brahmanical social order. During this period of decline, departing monks concealed numerous statues and images under the soil, and heaps of ashes were scattered amidst the ruins, indicating that the monasteries had been destroyed by fire. The glory of Buddha Dhamma vanished suddenly, like a rainbow at sunset.

Shravasti appears to have been of great importance as a center of art and religion by the 3rd century AD. With the fall of the Kosala kingdom, Shravasti's wealth, opulence, religious, and political importance began to decline. When the Chinese traveler Fa-Hien visited this area, this city was almost deserted and only a settlement of 200 families remained there. Ancient monasteries, temples, pillars etc. all had started getting destroyed. Efforts were being made to build new monasteries and temples in their place. Only about two hundred years later, during the time of another Chinese traveler Hiuen Tsang, this city was almost depopulated and destroyed. He had written that only the boundary wall of the city was left and vegetation had grown on most of the buildings. Only the foundation of King Prasenjit's palace remained. Some temples were definitely surviving at that time, in which a few monks used to reside. In 632 AD, it was completely deserted.

There is evidence to show that some Buddhist establishments survived in Jetavana down to the middle of the 12th century. In 1130 AD, the last patrons of Jetavana were King Govindachandra of Kanauj and Banaras and his devout wife Kumaradevi. During a period of about 1600 years, Shravasti remained the center of Buddhism, associated with the ups and downs of a great religion.

The inscriptions and sculptures found in and near Shravasti indicate that it has existed since the time of the Buddha. It was an active Buddhist site and prosperous area until the 12th century. By the end of the 12th century, Shravasti remained a center of Buddhism, visited by large numbers of Buddhist monks and receiving royal patronage from the king of Kanauj.

After the 13th century AD, it was destroyed, deserted, and then covered with dunes and Shravasti disappeared into the depths of darkness until it was brought to light and identified with Shravasti by Sir Alexander Cunningham in 1862. In 1862, the whole area of the city, except few clearances near the gateway was a mass of almost impenetrable forests.

3. PEOPLE ASSOCIATED WITH SHRAVASTI

1. Anathapindika

Anathapindika was one of the prominent and devoted disciples of the Buddha. He was always ready to help everyone. Due to this virtue, Anathapindika was known as the *'Lord of Orphans'* in the history of Buddhism. Anathapindika was born into a wealthy merchant family in Shravasti, with the birth name Sudatta. He had invited the Buddha and his Bhikkhu Sangha to Shravasti, and he had built the huge Jetavana Vihara for them by spending a substantial amount of money.

Anathapindika's Life and Family

Sudatta, also known as Anathapindika, was the son of a wealthy merchant named Sumana from Shravasti. When Sudatta grew up, he married a woman named Punna-lakkhan, meaning *'one who has the mark of merit'*, who was the sister of a wealthy merchant of Rajagruha. Anathapindika had a son named Kala and three daughters: Maha-subhadda, Kula-subhadda, and Sumana. His daughter-in-law was Sujata, the youngest sister of Vishakha, one of the Buddha's patrons. Anathapindika was very happy with his family. His wife, Punnalakkhana, a well-behaved woman, used to take care of the servants and monks. Two of his daughters, Kula-Subhadda was disciples of the Buddha. Both had a high level of understanding of both the spiritual world and the material world. However, the youngest daughter Sumana, was highly intelligent and surpassed all the family members in her thinking. By listening to the Buddha and his teachings, she soon attained the second stage of the Dhamma path. Kala, the son of Anathapindaka, embraced the Dhamma through the teachings of the Buddha. Like his father, he also became prosperous and came to be known as *'Laghu Anathapindik'*. Like his father, Kala was very generous by nature and gave generously to the Buddha's Sangha. Kala was married to Vishakha's younger sister, Sujata. Kala was very happy with his family background and the wealth he received from both sides. However, Kala's wife Sujata was a very mean woman and her thoughts revolved around these small things, so she was unable to generate any good thoughts. She was dissatisfied, irritable and she used to express her unhappiness on others. She was behaving in a hostile and angry manner towards everyone. She used to beat her servants and spread fear and terror whenever she appeared. Nor did she follow the rules of decorum in her relations with her in-laws and husband. But the situation changed after listening to the Buddha's sermon.

Anathapindika met the Buddha

Buddhist literature describes Anathapindika's first meeting with the Buddha in Rajagruha. During his business, Anathapindika used to come to meet his brother-in-law Subhuti in Rajagruha. Subhuti was already a follower of the Buddha. When Anathapindika reached his brother-in-law's house, he saw preparations for a grand welcome for the Buddha and his Sangha at the house. When Anathapindika asked about the preparations, his brother-in-law Subhuti told him that they were preparing to meet the Buddha and his Sangha. Hearing this, Anathapindika was very happy and said,

"You mean that an Enlightened One has appeared in the world."

"Absolutely right, the Buddha is an Enlightened Guru. His personality is bright and inspiring. Tomorrow, you will get a chance to see the Exalted One."

He became intrigued and asked them for more details. Inspired by the descriptions, he expressed a deep desire to meet the Buddha in person. Sudatta's mind was filled with happiness and inspiration without any reason. A feeling of intense love and reverence for the Buddha was awakened in him. He became restless and wanted to meet the Buddha as soon as possible, without waiting until noon the next day.

That night, Anathapindika's excitement and eagerness to meet the Buddha were so intense that he couldn't sleep. That night, even after waking up three times and seeing that morning had not yet come, he got up, wore his clothes, and set out for Veluvana. As he made his way to Veluvana, a feeling of fear and hesitation momentarily overcame him. However, he composed himself and continued his journey. When he reached Veluvana, the first rays of the early morning sun were falling on the bamboo leaves.

Though he had come to see the Buddha, he still felt a sense of nervousness. At the same time, the Buddha was passing by while walking in meditation. Anathapindika approached the Buddha, folded his hands, saluted him and followed the Buddha. He told the Buddha how eagerly and desperately he had spent the whole night to see him. He said to the Buddha,

"I wish to receive the teachings of your Saddhamma path."

The Buddha then delivered a discourse to him. In this teaching, the Buddha spoke about the *gradual path* which included topics such as generosity (*dana*), moral conduct (*sila*), and the benefits of renunciation (*nekkhamma*). Hearing the Buddha's words, Anathapindika experienced deep joy and insight. Sudatta was very pleased and requested him to make him his devotee too. Knowing this desire, the Buddha blessed him with goodwill and love. He immediately became a stream-enterer (*sotapanna*), which is the first stage of enlightenment in the Buddhist path.

On the same day at noon, when Anathapindika heard the Buddha's sermon at his brother-in-law's residence, he became overjoyed. He bowed before the Buddha and said,

"Acharya, till now the people of Magadh Kingdom have learned about you and your Sangha. However, people of Shravasti did not get the opportunity to welcome you and receive the teachings of Saddhamma. I invite you to come and stay in Kosal Rajya for a few days."

The Buddha said that he would take the decision after consulting his senior disciples.

A few days later, when Sudatta came to Veluvana again, he got the good news that the Buddha had accepted the invitation to come to Shravasti.

The Buddha asked Sudatta, whether Shravasti had a suitable place for the Bhikkhu Sangha to stay. Sudatta said,

"Lord, I will arrange nice accommodation for you and the Bhikkhu Sangha."

Sudatta also suggested that Sariputta be allowed to accompany him so that he could supervise the arrangements for your stay.

After asking Sariputta, the Buddha agreed to take him along.

After a week, Sudatta and Sariputta left together from Rajagruha for Shravasti and after crossing the river Ganga, they started traveling towards Vaishali. In Vaishali, they met Amrapali and stayed for the night at Amravan (mango orchard). Sariputta told Amrapali that the Tathagata Buddha would pass through Vaishali with his group of monks in the next six months. Amrapali said that it would be a privilege for her to welcome the Tathagata Buddha and his Sangha.

After taking leave from Amrapali, both of them reached Shravasti in a month along the banks of the river Achiravati (Rapti).

Kosala was a big and prosperous state, and was as powerful as the Magadha state. Sudatta invited Sariputta to his residence for a meal. Sudatta introduced his parents and all other family members to him.

Bhante Sariputta used to beg alms in the city every morning and sleep at night in forests on the river bank.

Purchase of Jetavana From Prince Jeta

Sudatta started searching for a suitable place for Buddha and his Sangha to stay. Jeta's garden seemed to be more suitable for Sudatta than all other places. The garden was neither too close nor too far from the city. The place was such that it would not be occupied by people during the day nor would there be noise at night. Sudatta thought that if he could get that garden, then Buddha and his Sangh could stay there. Sudatta went to meet Prince Jeta and requested him to sell the garden.

Sudatta said,

"Prince Jetta, I have invited Buddha and his Sangh here in Shravasti, and I am searching for a suitable place for their stay and to deliver dhamma discourses. The Jetavana garden you own is close to the city and the most ideal place for the construction of monasteries for Buddha and his Sangha. I need Jetavana to accommodate them."

This garden was gifted to Prince Jeta by his father, King Prasenjit. Prince Jeta said,

"I love this garden very much. I cannot even think of selling it."

"Seth ji, if you want Jetavana, I can sell it on one condition. If you spread the entire garden with gold coins, then the gold will be mine, and Jetavana will be yours."

Sudatta said,

"Price Jetta, I accept this condition. Tomorrow, I will arrange for gold coins for this purpose."

When Prince Jetta realized Sudatta's determination to purchase the Jetavana, he said,

"I was just joking. Actually, I don't want to sell this beautiful park at all. Please don't bother to bring gold coins here tomorrow."

Sudatta said resolutely,

"You are a prince, you must keep your word. You cannot go back on your word."

Prince Jeta agreed, thinking that Sudatta would not be able to gather so many gold coins. Next morning, Sudatta loaded the gold coins in carts and brought them to the forests of Prince Jeta and asked the servants to spread the gold coins over the entire surface of the garden.

Prince Jeta was stunned to see so many gold coins. He started wondering who this Gautam Buddha, for whom Seth Sudatta was making such a big sacrifice.

When he asked Sudatta, the latter said,

"I can even give my life for them. Buddha has honoured the entire Shravasti by accepting my invitation. He is an embodiment of compassion, sacrifice and welfare. His teachings can change many human lives."

Prince Jeta was greatly impressed by whatever Sudatta said about Gautam Buddha.

Hearing this, Prince Jeta said,

"If you are making such a sacrifice by spending your precious wealth for the purchase of the land for the construction of a monastery, then I would be the first person to gift this garden to you for such a holy work. I request you to take all the gold coins, as I donate this park to you free of cost. Now, Jetavana is yours."

Sudatta said,

"I cannot take these gold coins back."

The Prince Jeta said,

"For me to accept these gold coins would be an insult to a great man like you. If you cannot take these coins back, then use this wealth to build a Sangha-Vihar for Buddhist monks."

Both Sudatta and Prince Jeta decided to construct monasteries for Buddha and his Sangha. Sariputta, Prince Jeta and Anathapindika supervised the construction periodically.

After four months, the Vihar was almost ready. After the completion of the Jetavana monastery, Sariputra left for Rajagriha to invite Buddha and the Bhikkhu Sangha to Shravasti.

Before the start of the journey to Shravasti, Buddha told Sariputta that the Sangha would be in Veluvana under the leadership of Kaundanna and Urubela Kashyapa, while the remaining three hundred bhikkhus would accompany him to Shravasti.

When the Buddha and his entourage arrived at Shravasti, Sudatta and Prince Jeta welcomed them and escorted them to the Vihara. Impressed by the well-arranged Jetavana, Buddha praised Sudatta, saying, "The bhikkhus would be protected from wild animals, snakes, mosquitoes, and rain. Bhikkhus would come to this monastery from all directions. I am sure you will also become a Saddhamma in the same way. You will follow the righteous path in life."

Sudatta said,

"This is the result of the hard work of Sariputta and Prince Jeta."

Shramana Rahul also came to Shravasti with the Buddha. He was just twelve years old. After arriving at Jetavana, he resumed his education under Sariputta. Sixty new monks joined the Sangha at Shravasti. The rainy season was approaching.

Tathagata Buddha entered Jetavana in the fourteenth year of the first rainy season of his Bodhi. Therefore, Jetavana must have been constructed between 510-508 AD.

Anathapindika continued to generously support the Buddha and his Sangha throughout his life. As the Chief Patron, Anathapindika used to feed a large number of monks daily. He ensured a regular supply of clothing and food to the Jetavana Monastery. He also facilitated meetings between lay disciples and the Buddha. He served as one of the Buddha's primary disciples.

Whenever the Buddha was in Shravasti, Anathapindika used to visit him twice a day. After meeting the Buddha for the first time, Anathapindika committed himself to follow the Buddha's teachings and also encouraged his family, friends, employees, and everyone around him to do the same. When Anathapindika was away from home for some professional activity, his eldest daughter Sumana used to look after the Bhikkhu Sangha. She helped her father with his daily religious activities. Naturally, Anathapindika was very happy with his daughter. But it is said that who has control over time?

Once, Sumana fell seriously ill. Despite extensive treatment, she could not recover and passed away. Before her death, she had started addressing her father as 'Brother'. Anathapindika was deeply saddened by the death of his daughter. He was even more saddened by the thought that before her death, she had called him 'Brother'. He felt that his daughter had not lost her mental balance before she died. He was unable to understand how this had happened.

With a heavy heart, he approached the Buddha, paid his respects, and sat in front of him. Seeing his expression, the Buddha asked him why he looked so upset. Then, Anathapindika explained the reason. Hearing his problem, Buddha explained to him, "Anathapindika! You don't need to worry. Your daughter had not lost her mental balance. She was one step ahead of you on the spiritual path. "Therefore, if she addressed you as 'Brother', you should not feel bad about it."

Hearing this, Anathapindika understood the matter, and his sorrow went away.

Death of Anathapindika

When Anathapindika fell ill, Buddha's two chief disciples, Bhikkhu Sariputta and Ananda, visited him. Bhante Sariputta taught the Dhamma teaching which was not being given to the common people.He appreciated it so much that he requested Sariputta and Ananda to teach these same truths to other lay disciples as well. After

Sariputta and Ananda left him, Anathapindika passed away peacefully experiencing deep joy from the wisdom he had attained.

Lesson from Anathpindika's life

Anathapindika is considered to be one of the most generous disciples of the Buddha. He not only regularly provided alms and necessities to the Buddhist monks at Jetavana, but also invited hundreds of monks to his residence for meals every day. Referring to Anathapindika's support of the Buddha and his bhikkhu Sangha, the Buddha said that for a person who is dedicated to perfecting the virtue of generosity, nothing in the world can stop them from giving and helping others. Anathapindika's habit of generosity coupled with some misfortunes, transformed him from a rich man to a poor man at one time. But even in times of difficulty, Anathapindika continued his virtues of generosity and patronage to Buddhism, although in a much more humble manner. Later, due to his patience, honest efforts in business, and the power of generosity, he eventually acquired wealth again.

Anathapindika's patronage had a significant impact on Buddhism. Anathapindika's generosity also inspired King Prasenjit to begin patronizing Buddhism. After Vishakha built the Migaramata Pasada monastery at Shravasti, the Buddha also used the monastery of Anathapindika and the monastery of Vishakha alternatively whenever he stayed in Shravasti.

According to religious studies scholar Todd Lewis, Anathapindika was one of the most popular figures in Buddhist art and story in the Asian Buddhist tradition. Buddhist scholars George D. Bond and W.P. Guruge cited Anathapindika's story as evidence that the Buddhist path for ordinary people and acts of generosity in Buddhism are not separate from the path towards Nirvana. Due to Anathapindika's support to the Bhikkhu Sangha, the Buddha was able to spend approximately twenty-five rainy seasons with the Sangha at Shravasti, the longest period at any one place during the Buddha's lifetime. Therefore, Shravasti was considered a major center of Buddhism as the Buddha gave most of the Dhamma sermons here.

2. Angulimala

About 500 years before Christ, an astrologer in Shravasti had predicted that a Brahmin boy, due to his violent nature, could become a murderous robber. The parents named him 'Ahinsak'. Ahinsak was a very talented student and was also a favorite of his teacher, Acharya. Success generated jealousy among his fellow students. Some jealous classmates turned Acharya against Ahinsak by telling false things about him.

It so happened that shortly after, Ahinsak's studies ended, and he was preparing to go home. Then the teacher called him and said:

"My dear Ahinsak, one who has completed his studies has a duty to give a gift of respect to his teacher. So give me some gift to me!" — "Of course, master! What should I give?" — "You must bring me a thousand human little fingers of the right hand. This will be your final formal dedication to the studies you have completed."

The teacher probably hoped that Ahinsak, in attempting to accomplish that task, would himself be killed or, if captured by the king's men, would suffer the supreme punishment of hanging.

Faced with such an insulting demand, Ahinsak was the first to say,

"O Master! How can I do that? My family has never been involved in violence. They are harmless people." However, I have to follow the orders of the revered Guru."

Now Ahinsak agreed, and after paying due respect to his teacher, he went away to accomplish the wish of his guru.

To fulfill the wish of the revered Guru, he equipped himself with a set of five types of weapons and went to the wild Jalini forest in his home kingdom, Kosala. There he lived on a high rock from where he could observe the road below. When he saw the travelers coming, he would quickly descend, kill them and take a finger from each of his victims.

First, he hung the fingers on a tree where birds ate the meat and dropped the bones. When he saw that the bones were rotting on the ground, he put the fingers on a string and wore them as a garland. This act earned him the nickname Angulimala, 'A man with the finger-garland.'

The robber had vowed to wear a rosary of a thousand fingers. After killing 999 people, he cut off their fingers and made a rosary from those fingers. He was now looking for the 1000th finger.

Buddha Meets Angulimala

Buddha returned to Shravasti and started living in Jetavana. One morning when Buddha went out of the city to seek alms in Shravasti, he saw that the streets were deserted, all the people were sitting locked in their houses. Buddha stood in front of the house from where he used to get alms. The people of the house opened the door a little and saw that Buddha was standing outside. The owner of the house came out and requested Buddha to come inside. As soon as Buddha entered the house, the owner of the house locked the door and requested Buddha to sit down and have his meal inside. He said, "Sir, it is very dangerous to go out today. Killer Angulimala has been seen in this area. Whenever he kills someone, he cuts off one of the victim's fingers and wears it as a necklace around his neck. The surprising thing is that the person he killed did not have anything stolen from them. King Prasenjit has deployed several squads of soldiers and police to capture him, but the army failed to capture him,"

Buddha asked, "What was the need to appoint so many soldiers and police to arrest one person?"

"Respected Buddha, Angulimala is a very dangerous robber. He has amazing fighting skills. Once he surrounded a group of people on the road and killed most of them. Angulimala lives in the Jalini forest, and no one dares to pass through it without harm and fear. A few days ago, twenty armed soldiers had entered the forest to arrest him, but only two of them could return safely. Now, he has been seen in this city. Therefore, no one goes out for any work."

After getting information about Angulimala, Buddha stood up and took leave. All family members of the house tried to persuade Buddha to remain inside, but Buddha did not agree. The villagers also tried to stop Buddha, but Buddha did not agree. He said that he would be able to maintain people's trust in him only if he continued to beg normally.

When the Buddha was walking slowly on the forest path in a conscious state, the sound of a person running was heard from a distance. He understood that it was Angulimala. Buddha's mind was moving forward in a state of full awareness of whatever was happening. Angulimala lived on the top of a hill. He saw a beautiful man coming.

He said, "Okay, this is my 1000th prey."

So, he laughed loudly and made noise, saying - "Stop, I am coming." Buddha continued walking with his slow and serious steps. From the arc of his footsteps, it was understood that Angulimala had started walking fast instead of running and was not far away from him. Although Buddha was fifty-six years old, his eyesight and hearing power were sharp. He had nothing in his hand except an alms bowl. Buddha had understood that Angulimala had come very close and he had a sword in his hand.

Buddha continued walking smoothly.

Angulimala shouted, "Bhikkhu, stop."

Walking fast, Angulimala came near the Buddha and said, "Bhikkhu, I told you to stop, why didn't you stop?"

Buddha smiled and said, "I don't know how long I have been standing, only you have been running."

Angulimala said,

"You are not afraid of me. The whole country of Kosala is afraid of me. I am the most powerful. I will kill you."

Buddha spoke fearlessly,

"How can I accept that you are the most powerful person in the kingdom? You will have to prove this."

Angulimala said, "Okay."

Buddha said-

"You break a branch of that tree."

Angulimala broke the branch.

Buddha said- "Now put this branch back on the tree."

Angulimala said- "Does a broken branch grow back?"

Buddha said-

"When you can't put a branch back together, how did you become the most powerful? If you cannot give life to someone, then you have no right to give him death."

Hearing this, Angulimala was shocked, and the words of Buddha awakened a feeling of compassion within him.

Angulimala had never encountered such a person who was so bright and easygoing. Everyone used to run away in fear of him. Why was this bhikkhu not feeling any kind of fear?

Buddha was looking at him with friendship and compassion, as if he were a friend or brother. Angulimala could no longer bear the kind and virtuous gaze of Buddha and said,

"Bhikkhu, you said that you have become silent a long time ago, you have stopped long ago, but you are still walking. You said that I am not the only one who has stopped. What did you mean by this?"

The Buddha replied,

"Angulimala, I have long ago stopped doing things that cause harm to others. I have learned to protect not only humans but all living beings.

Angulimala, all living beings love their lives. Everyone fears death; we feel scared. We should develop a compassionate heart and a feeling of protecting all living beings."

Angulimala said,

"Humans do not love humans, then why should I love other people? Humans are cruel and deceitful."

Buddha said simply,

"Angulimala, you have had to suffer a lot at the hands of people. Sometimes humans become very cruel. This cruelty is due to ignorance, hatred, and malice. Not all people are cruel. People are also intelligent and full of compassion. My Saddhamma path transforms cruelty into compassion."

Angulimala was greatly impressed by the words of the Buddha. He thought that this was Buddha.

Angulimala asked, "Are you the monk Gautam Buddha?"

Buddha nodded his approval with a smile.

Angulimala said,

"How unfortunate that I have not met you before. I have gone too far on the path of destruction. Now, it is not possible for me to return to that place."

Buddha said,

"Angulimala, all times are right to do good work. Stop walking on the path of violence and hatred. Suffering is vast, but if you look back, you will see the shore."

Angulimala said,

"Gautama, I cannot turn back even if I want to, after that no one will let me live peacefully."

The Buddha took hold of Angulimala's hand and said,

"Angulimala, if you give up your hatred and practice the path of Saddhamma, I will protect you. I have not the slightest doubt that you will be able to succeed on the path to Nirvana."

Angulimala bowed before the Buddha. He untied the sword tied on his back and placed it on the ground, then prostrated himself at the feet of the Buddha. After a long time, he raised his head and said to the Buddha:

"I vow to give up the evil path. I will follow you and learn the path of compassion from you. I beg you to make me your disciple."

At the same time, Sariputta, Ananda, Upali, Kambal and other bhikkhus also reached the spot. They surrounded the Buddha and Angulimala. The Buddha asked Ananda to give him the robe and other clothes. They removed the hair from Angulimala's head. Angulimala was immediately given the pravrajya by Upali, a well-known bhikkhu of the Sangha who had compiled the Vinaya Pitaka later.

He bowed to everyone and chanted the three gems:

"Buddham Sharanan Gachchami,

Dhammam Sharanan Gachchami,

Sangham Sharanan Gachchami."

With him, they all returned to Jetavana. Other disciples started saying to the Buddha, Bhante, he is a trickster. He has come here only to show that he has changed now, but his trick would kill us all.

Gautam Buddha said,

"No, now he has become my disciple like you. All the sins he has committed have gone away, and now he is an innocent man."

For the next ten days, Upali and Sariputta taught him sheela, taught him meditation and explained the method of begging. Angulimala tried to learn everything with full dedication.

When Buddha met Angulimala after two weeks, he was astonished to see Angulimala's progress. The radiance of gentleness and a stable mind was visible in Angulimala.

Now, Gautam Buddha asked Ahinsak to go to the village from where he had killed his people. When he went there, the small child gave alms to the innocent, non-violent person. When he accepted the alms, he said to the child in compassionate words,

"Son, may your parents' protection and blessings be upon you."

Hearing this, the child started crying. Bhante Ahinsak asked the child, "Why are you crying?"

The small child said that his parents were killed by Angulimala and now his parents are no longer in this world.

Feeling sad after hearing this, Bhante Ahinsak came non-violently and fell at the feet of the Buddha, and said, "I am very sad, I am a great sinner."

Bhante Ahinsak felt very sad remembering his past deeds.

One day, Buddha went to Shravasti for alms, along many bhikkhus including Angulimala. At the city gate, he saw King Prasenjit riding on a horse with a group of soldiers. The king and the army generals were fully prepared for war. When the king saw Buddha, he dismounted from his horse and bowed to Buddha.

The Buddha asked,

"Your Majesty, has something happened? Has the army of another king attacked your kingdom?"

The king replied,

"No one has attacked Kosal. I have gathered these soldiers to catch the murderer Angulimala. He is a very dangerous person. Till now, no one has been able to catch him. Two weeks ago, he was seen near the city. My people are still haunted by the fear of him."

Buddha said,

"Do you believe that Angulimala is so terrible?"

The king said,

"Bodhisattva, Angulimala is a great danger to every man, woman, and child. I will not rest until I kill him."

The Buddha asked,

"If Angulimala repents of his actions and promises never to kill again, if he becomes a bhikkhu and begins to respect all living beings, will there still be a need to capture him and punish him?"

The Buddha pointed to Bhante Ahinsak who was standing behind him and said,

"This bhikkhu is none other than Angulimala."

When King Prasenjit found the terrible murderer standing so close to him, he became terrified.

Buddha said,

"Now, there is no need to be afraid of him. Now we call him Ahinsak - non-violent."

The King bowed to the new Bhikkhu Ahinsak.

He then addressed the Buddha and said,

"Bodhisattva, your brilliance is truly wonderful. You have established peace and harmony in situations which no one else has been able to do. What others have not been able to do through force and violence, you have achieved. This has been made possible by your great compassion. Please accept my heartfelt gratitude."

King Prasenjit continued,

"Guruvarya! If Angulimala has become your disciple, and has given up violence and adopted modesty and is leading a pure and harmless life of a monk, then there is no limit to my happiness. I will provide him with clothing and food."

The news of Angulimala becoming a Bhikkhu spread rapidly throughout the city. Everyone heaved a sigh of relief. The news of the murderer's change of heart also became known to the neighboring states. Due to this, the prestige of the Buddha and the Sangha increased further.

Once Bhante Ahinsak went to his own town to beg for alms, and some people there recognized him. They were not aware that Angulimala had now become non-violent again. So they attacked him as soon as they recognized him. Within some time, a crowd gathered there. Everyone started beating him with fists, sticks, and stones with the intention to kill him. Ahinsak kept on getting beaten silently. He didn't say anything to anyone. Because now he had changed.

Everyone left Ahinsak half-dead to die a gruesome death. After regaining consciousness, Ahinsak somehow reached Gautam Buddha. Then Gautam Buddha asked Ahinsak,

"Didn't you get angry when everyone was beating you?"

To this Ahimsak replied,

"No, when I killed people I was not aware of what I was doing. Similarly, when they were beating me today, they also did not know that I had changed and they were doing wrong."

Saying this, Ahinsak sacrificed his life.

Lesson from Angulimala's Life

The story of Angulimala is one of the most famous stories in Buddhist literature, not only in modern times but also in ancient times. Two important Chinese pilgrims who traveled to India told the story and about the places they saw that were associated with the life of Angulimala. From a Buddhist perspective, the story of Angulimala serves as an example that even the worst people can overcome their mistakes and return to the right path. This story is the best example of good karma destroying bad karma. Buddhists widely regard Angulimala as a symbol of complete transformation and as a demonstration that the Buddhist path can transform even the least likely initiates. Buddhists have been taught this story of Angulimala as an example of the Buddha's compassion and supernatural accomplishment. The conversion of Angulimala has been cited as evidence of the Buddha's abilities as a teacher and as an example of the healing power of the Buddha's teachings.

The story of Angulimala demonstrates how criminals are influenced by their psychosocial and physical environment. The story of Angulimala has implications for the justice system. In Buddhist ethics, criminals should be given a chance to improve their character. If a criminal like Angulimala has already reformed himself, there is no need to punish him. The story of Angulimala is one of transformative justice and rehabilitation of humanity.

The story of Angulimala teaches that even the most extreme circumstances can awaken the potential for enlightenment, that people can and do change, and that people are best influenced through persuasion. This story should inspire every person, showing that they can change even in adverse circumstances and attain enlightenment. It also shows that people can be motivated by compassion rather than punishment or coercion.

Angulimala is an important figure in Buddhist literature, portrayed as a ruthless robber who was completely transformed from a ruthless robber and murderer to a Buddhist Bhikkhu. Angulimala is considered a symbol of spiritual transformation and his story is a lesson that everyone can change their life for the better if shown the right path.

3. Queen Mallika

The extraordinary story of Mallika, a gardener's daughter becoming the chief queen of the kingdoms of Kashi and Kosal, is truly fascinating. A garland maker in Shravasti named his fair, slim and lovely daughter Mallika. She was smart and polite since childhood. At the age of sixteen, one day she went with her friends to the public flower gardens and carried three portions of fermented rice in her basket as sustenance for the day.

As she was leaving the city gate, a group of monks from the monastery situated on the hill came to collect alms in the city. The chief of their guild was standing outside, whose grandeur and sublime beauty so impressed her that she felt she should let them eat all the food she possessed in her basket. She was immediately filled with a deep feeling of fulfillment and joy. Overjoyed, she bent down and touched the feet of the Bhikkhu with reverence. The bhikkhu also smiled softly in blessing. She did not know that the Bhikkhu who radiated sublime peace and joy was none other than the Buddha himself.

Buddha smiled. Ananda, his attendant, knew that a fully enlightened person does not smile without reason. therefore, he asked Buddha, "Why was he smiling?" Buddha replied, "This girl would soon take advantage of her gift by becoming the queen of Kosala kingdom."

That afternoon, her heart filled with a feeling of happiness and she started dancing on a cloud of happiness. The young horseman Prasenjit, King of Kosala, was defeated in a battle with Ajatashatru, the powerful King of Magadha. Defeated in the battle and forced to retreat, Prasenjit was distressed and dejected on his way back to his palace at Shravasti. He was attracted by the melody of the girl's song. A coating of cool peace spread over his aching heart. He looked around the garden with great joy and saw a beautiful young girl dancing as well as singing. He spontaneously moved towards the singing and dancing girl, oblivious of the world around her. He was struck by the innocent face of the cheerful, bright girl.

As the tired stranger approached her, Mallika was not afraid; instead, she took the reins of the horse and looked him straight in the eyes. She saw the tiredness in his eyes and helped the rider to get down and lie down near the grove. Mallika rubbed his feet with a piece of wet cloth and gently fanned him. As soon as she did this, the young man fell asleep. When he woke up after a while, he looked deeply into her face and asked who she was and whether she was married or not. Mallika shyly replied, "No. For some time, the Kosala king observed Mallika, who was a vision of beauty and grace. He talked to her about his misfortune in the war. Pleased by her consoling words and charmed by her beauty and gentleness, the Kosala king decided to make her his queen.

Carefully placing her on his horse, he took her back to her parents' home. He obtained the consent of her parents to marry their daughter to him and make her the queen of Kosala. In the evening, King Prasenjit sent some people to her parents to bring Mallika with great fanfare. He made her his wife and chief queen of the Kosala kingdom.

Being the queen of the king of Kosala, Mallika was respected by all and was surrounded by luxuries and numerous servants who fulfilled her every wish. She demonstrated her gentleness by serving her husband with the five virtues of an ideal wife, namely: always getting up before her husband woke up, and going to bed after him, always obeying his commands, always being submissive, and only using kind words. Her personal qualities were praised by wise men, servants, subjects, monks, and the Buddha himself.

After her very blissful married life, suddenly a new challenge in her married life arrived as King Prasenjit decided to go for a second marriage. This was a big challenge for her, and she had to prove that she too was free from jealousy. The King married Buddha's cousin. Although it is said that it is in the nature of a person not to allow their rival into their home, Mallika, however, welcomed the king's second wife with open arms and treated her like a real sister without any ill will and both started living peacefully.

In due course, his second wife Vasabha gave birth to a son, who was to be the crown prince, and Princess Vaziri was born to Prasenjit's chief queen Mallika. Yet, Mallika was not jealous of Vasabha, but was happy with Vasabha's good fortune.

While King Prasenajit was with the Buddha, he received news that his wife Queen Mallika had given birth to a daughter. The king was not happy with this news because he wanted a son. When the king expressed disappointment over the birth of a daughter, the Buddha told him that a woman is superior to a man if she is clever, virtuous, well-behaved, and loyal. A girl with good values can uplift the family and train her children and future generations to become virtuous people. Mother's contribution in grooming and moulding the character of future generations is indeed significant. Then she can become the wife of a great king and give birth to an almighty ruler. The Buddha advised King Prasenjit to love his daughter without any undue attachment or prejudice and to inculcate good values in her. When the daughter, Princess Vaziri grew up, she became queen of Magadha and thus, the ancestor of the greatest Indian emperor Ashoka, who ruled Magadha 250 years later.

Mallika became a devoted follower of the Buddha and a supporter of the Sangha. She was also an insightful queen who questioned and analyzed every word spoken by the Buddha. Observing the diverse socio-economic status of people in society and their progression from poverty to wealth and power, she convinced herself that nothing occurs without a reason. To comprehend this phenomenon, Mallika visited Jetavana Monastery to meet the Buddha with the following questions;

- Why are some women beautiful, rich and powerful?
- While some are beautiful, yet lack wealth and power.
- Others are ugly, but rich and powerful.
- Some are ugly, poor and powerless?

The Buddha explained to her that all the virtues and ways of life of people everywhere depend on their moral purity (śīlā). Beauty comes from a person's gentle and forgiving nature. Prosperity arises from generosity of heart and the roots of skill and power lie in not being jealous of others, but rejoicing in their success and always supporting their qualities. Very rarely, all three qualities are manifested in a person; and when that happens that person becomes beautiful, wealthy and powerful.

At the end of the Buddha's discourse, she took refuge in the Buddha, the Dhamma, and the Sangha and remained a faithful disciple for the rest of her life. Mallika, after hearing this discourse of the Buddha, resolved in her heart that she would always be gentle towards her subjects and would never scold them, would give alms to all monks, brahmins and the poor and would never be jealous of anyone who was happy. Queen Mallika's excellent management of her royal household, her humility in serving her husband and her sense of friendliness and compassion towards her servants all contributed to her admirable personality.

Once, King Prasenjit requested the Buddha to teach the Dhamma to his two queens. At the King's request, the Buddha appointed his close disciple and cousin Bhante Ananda to teach the two queens. It is said that Queen Mallika understood and learned the teachings easily, whereas Queen Vasabha, Prasenjit's second wife, struggled to concentrate and had difficulty in learning. This suggests that Queen Mallika was a dedicated, honest, hardworking and intelligent woman.

As the queen of the Kosala kingdom, she enjoyed a position of respect and authority. Her common sense, generosity of heart and genuine desire to help the poor were all profound. She also implemented the Dhamma teachings of her teacher, the Buddha for the benefit of the people in the kingdom. She tried to shower love, understanding, kindness and harmony upon her family and the public alike. She exercised considerable influence in shaping the King's attitude and policies towards their subjects and was largely successful in bringing about some vital changes in the state. Queen Mallika demonstrated generosity by helping the poor, donating food to monks and building a large hall in her private garden 'Mallikaram' to hold Dhamma discussions.

Death of Queen Mallika

Mallika died suddenly. The news of her death reached King Prasenjit when he was listening to the Buddha's sermon. He was in deep shock and inconsolable grief. The Buddha attempted to console him by saying:

"All beings are mortal, they end with death,

they have the nature of death.

All the utensils made by the potter,

whether ripe or raw, they are fragile and likely to break.

They are broken up at the end."

The Buddha told the King about the inevitability of old age and death. By understanding the impermanence of all that comes into existence, which has a death and decay, one can reduce suffering. King Prasenjit of Kosala was thus consoled, strengthened his mind and then left Jetavana peacefully.

4. King Prasenjit

In those days, there were three major cities in the Kosal region, namely Ayodhya, Saket and Shravasti as well as many other smaller cities like Setavya, Ukattha, Dandakappa, Nalakapana and Pankadha. Shravasti was recorded as the capital of the Kosal Kingdom during the Mahajanapada period (6th–5th century BCE). These kingdoms contributed to the advancements of science, astronomy, religion and philosophy in ancient India and hence it is called the Indian Golden Age. Kosal had a particularly close connection with the life of the Buddha, as he had spent 25 rainy seasons in Shravasti.

The Mahakosal King Prasenjit ruled the kingdoms of Kashi and Kosal (modern Awadh) in the 6th century BCE. Prasenjit was a contemporary of the Buddha. He respected the Shakya dynasty in which the Buddha was born. Prasenjit studied in Takshashila in his early life. King Prasenjit was the ruler of the Kosala Kingdom and the brother of Kosala Devi, the wife of King Bimbisara. Prasenjit fought continuously with Ajatashatru, the king of Magadha. Prasenjit hated Ajatashatru because of the murder of his brother-in-law, Bimbisara.

His sister, Kosala Devi, died of grief. Prasenjit confiscated the bride's gift of a prosperous village called Kosaladevi in Kashi. This sparked hostilities between the Kosal and Magadh kingdoms, which continued for a long time.

Ajatashatru was the first to dominate and drove Prasenjit to Shravasti. Eventually, Ajatashatru was trapped and had to surrender his entire army. Peace was established and Prasenjit returned back Ajatashatru's army, freedom and the disputed village in Kashi and also married his daughter Waziri to him.

King Prasenjit became a devout listener of the Buddha's discourses, while his queen, Mallika and her two sisters, Soma and Sakula, followed them curiously. At the insistence of his wife Mallika, Prasenjit became a follower of Shakyamuni Buddha and attempted to protect and support the Buddhist sect. He often visited the Buddha whenever the Buddha lived in Shravasti and around the vicinity.

According to the Agama Sutra, shortly after Shakyamuni Buddha attained enlightenment, Prasenjit ascended the throne and wished to take wife from the Sakya, the rulers from whom Shakyamuni Buddha came and whose people were considered to be of noble birth. A man named Mahanama, a member of the Sakyas, married the king to his maid's beautiful daughter, falsely claiming that she was his own daughter. From her was born a prince, who was named Virudhak. When Virudhak was eight years old, he went to Kapilvastu, the realm of the Sakyas, where he was told the truth behind his birth and thus was put to shame. Later, when he ascended the throne, this led him to destroy the vast majority of the Sakyas kingdom.

When King Prasenjit came to know about Anathapindika's generosity, he wanted to emulate him and thus, he decided to donate food to five hundred monks every day. One day, when he came to know from his servants that the Bhikkhus were taking food from them and giving it to their followers in the city, the king was surprised, because he had always provided very tasty food to the monks, and so he asked the Buddha the reason for the monks' behavior. The Buddha explained to the king that the courtiers in the palace distributed food without any genuine feeling, as if they were laborers cleaning a barn or feeding thieves. They lacked faith and had no love for the monks while distributing food to the monks. Many of them also said that the Buddhist monks were lazy. When anything was given with that ill-will, no one could feel good even when receiving the most expensive food. On the other hand, loyal householders like Anathapindika and Vishakha in the city, they consider monks as their spiritual friends who used to work for the welfare and benefit of all beings. A humble meal provided by a friend will be more valuable than the most luxurious meal maliciously provided by someone who is indifferent or does not give in the right spirit. The generosity of Anathapindika and Vishakha also inspired King Prasenajit to begin generous patronage of Buddhism.

Hearing this, King Prasenjit of Kosal understood that the Buddha was indeed a wise teacher and decided to become his follower. King Prasenjit always sought the Buddha's advice on any issue. Even during his official duties, he found time to visit and talk to the Buddha.

Death of King Prasenjit

King Prasenjit did not die peacefully in his kingdom, but faced a tragic end. He did not die in his kingdom, but in a public place like a Dharamshala in Rajagruha.

Once, King Prasenjit went to the Buddha to listen to a discourse on the Dhamma. The king left his royal crown with the Commander Karayan before entering Jetavana to meet the Buddha. When King Prasenjit came out of Jetavana after meeting the Buddha, he was surprised to see only one chariot instead of four. At that place, he had left four chariots along with Commander Karayan and the charioteers. The Commander Karayan saw this as an opportunity and ran away with the king's crown. The charioteer told King Prasenjit that the Commander had taken the other three chariots to Shravasti.

The Commander approached the prince and appealed to him to become the king of Kosal. The Commander said,

"O Prince of Kosal, look, King Prasenjit has grown old and is now unable to handle the affairs of the kingdom. Therefore, I request you to become the king of Kosal."

The prince expressed his inability to become the king of Kosal while his father was alive. The Commander Karayan said to him furiously, "Look, I have the royal crown of Kosal, and if you reject my offer to become the king of Kosal, I will not miss this opportunity to become the king."

The Prince considered this very reluctantly and accepted the proposal of Commander Karayan to become the King of Kosal.

When King Prasenjit learned about the rebellion by his Prince son Virudhak with the help of Commander Karayan, he started feeling very disappointed and dejected. He became sad. He was unable to think what to do at that time. He considered various methods and their advantages and disadvantages.

However, he decided to approach King Ajatashatru of Magadh and his son-in-law to ask for help in countering the rebellion in the kingdom. He was feeling so dejected that, during the entire journey from Shravasti to Rajgruha, he drank only water and did not take even a single grain of food. He reached Rajgruha around midnight. He thought it would be better not to trouble King Ajatashatru for opening the palace doors at this odd time. He decided to rest at Dharamshala, a common public place on the outskirts of Rajgruha. That night, he fell seriously ill and there was no way to seek medical help at that odd hour of the night. He died in his eightieth year on the lap of his charioteer. Early in the morning, King Ajatashatru learned about the tragic death of his father-in-law, the King of Kosal. He performed the last rites with full royal honors.

Angered by the death of his father-in-law, the king of Kosal, Ajatashatru decided to teach a lesson to Prince Virudhak by dethroning him. He wanted to send his army to Shravasti. However, Bhante Vimal Kaudanya (Jivaka) discouraged him from doing so, saying that after all, the king had just died, and Prince Virudhak was now the natural heir to the kingdom of Kosal at Shravasti. King Ajatashatru heeded this advice, abandoned his plan to dethrone King Virudhak and accepted Virudhak as the king of Kosal.

When we assess the life of King Prasenjit, we learn many things from his life as a king and as an individual. King Prasenjit had a close association with the Buddha, and he sought the Buddha's advice on various matters including personal, political and spiritual concerns. This friendship and guidance helped the king navigate many of life's challenges. This teaches us the importance of seeking counsel from wise and knowledgeable people who can help guide us in difficult times, especially when it comes to moral and ethical decisions. Despite being a powerful king, Prasenjit showed humility and openness to the teachings of the Buddha. He was willing to question his own beliefs and policies, which eventually made him a more just and compassionate ruler. Leaders and individuals alike should be humble and open to learning, especially when confronted with new ideas or perspectives that challenge their previous beliefs.

Although King Prasenjit ruled a vast and powerful kingdom, his later years were marked by political instability and personal losses, including a temporary loss of his kingdom and the death of his beloved family members. This highlights the Buddhist teaching of impermanence (Anicca) and how power, wealth, and even relationships are transient. Understanding this can lead to greater wisdom, inner peace and emotional resilience. Prasenjit, influenced by the Buddha's teachings worked to ensure that his kingdom was governed with justice and compassion. His efforts to rule with morality reflected a deep concern for the welfare of his subjects.

5. Vishakha

Vishakha was a very attractive and independent-thinking woman. She had a perfect balance and a calm personality. She had her own ideas and believed in her convictions. Although her family was wealthy on both sides, she also ran her own business independently. She was known as an efficient manager, an effective speaker and an excellent communicator. Vishakha, also known as Migaramata, was a wealthy noblewoman. Vishakha was not only a major female disciple but also a major donor to the Bhikkhu Sangha of Gautam Buddha.

Her father was Dhananjay and her mother was Sumana. She was born in a distinguished and wealthy family in the town of Bhaddiya, which is currently known as Bhadaria near Bhagalpur in Bihar. When she was seven years old, the Buddha visited Bhaddiya with a large congregation of monks. Vishakha requested her grandfather Mendak that Gautam Buddha, the Guru of this world and the one who has immense kindness towards all living beings is coming to Bhaddiya city, and she wanted to bless her life with his darshaln. Please let her have his blessings. Grandfather Mendak was both surprised and overjoyed by the serious words of this little girl. He immediately said,

"Vishakha, is it such a simple thing, my granddaughter?"

He sent Vishakha with five hundred companions and chariots to see the Buddha. She stopped the chariots at some distance and walked to reach the Buddha. After a few days, Gautama Buddha, along with his Bhikkhu Sangha were invited for a meal by Mendak at his residence. After listening to the sermon of the Buddha, Vishakha attained Sotapanna, the first stage of the Buddhist spiritual path.

At that time, King Prasenjit was the king of Kosal Kingdom. When he heard about the respectable and generous nature of the Dhananjay family, he requested his brother-in-law, King Bimbisara of Magadha to send the family to Kosal, so that they could set a good example for the families in the Kosal kingdom. King Bimbisara forced the Dhananjay family to relocate from Magadha to the Kosal kingdom and made arrangements for their passage and accommodation. The family moved and settled in the city of Saket (present-day Ayodhya), where Dhananjay was given the job of treasurer by King Prasenjit. Vishakha grew up happily in her new residence at Saket with her family in a religious environment and engaged in family activities.

Vishakha's Wedding

In Shravasti, there was a prosperous family of a merchant named Migara, who had a son named Punnavardhan. While his parents were trying to arrange a marriage for Punnavardhan, he had no interest in getting married. When his parents kept pursuing him to get married, he informed them that he is ready to marry if they could find the most beautiful girl with certain characteristics, wit and wisdom. The parents sent a team of intelligent people around to search for a suitable girl. Wise people started searching for suitable girls as described by Punnavardhan in many cities.

On one occasion, the search team members saw Visakha going to the lake to take a bath on the day of the feast. At the same time, it was raining heavily. Vishakha's companions ran here and there for shelter, but Vishakha herself, walking at her usual pace, came to the place where the search team had already stopped to protect themselves from the rain. They observed that Vishakha was not running in search of nearby shelter, but she walked at a normal pace. They got upset over Vishakha's act. When she came to the shelter to protect herself from the rain, they criticized her as lazy for walking slowly and getting wet. However, the sixteen-year-old Vishakha explained politely to them that there are four people in the world for whom running is considered to be not suitable.

- The king in royal attire.
- The religious monk.
- A young girl.
- The royal elephants.

Furthermore, she also told them that she was afraid of slipping due to the rain and thus did not want to injure herself by running to escape the rain. Wet clothes could be dried, but if a woman of marriageable age met with an injury and if one of her body parts is broken, there may be a problem for her to marry and also a problem for her parents. During this conversation, the wise men observed that Vishakha possessed beauty as well as intelligence and had all the qualities that described by Punnavarddhan. The members of the search team were very impressed by her intelligence and clever answers. All the members approached Vishakha's family with a marriage proposal.

Both families agreed to the marriage. After the marriage, Vishakha went to Shravasti to live with her husband and in-laws. It is said that her father had appointed eight householders in Shravasti as Vishakha's facilitators or arbitrators, who would regularly inquire whether there were any complaints against Vishakha by her in-laws. When Vishakha reached Shravasti after the marriage, the people were amazed by her beauty and welcomed her with several precious gifts. Vishakha redistributed all the gifts received to the people of the city.

Vishakha's father-in-law Migara became a disciple

Vishakha's father-in-law Migara was a follower of Jainism and was not at all happy with his daughter-in-law being a follower of Buddha. Vishakha once requested her father-in-law to invite the Buddha and his Bhikkhus Sangha for a meal at his residence. But he was unwilling to invite the Buddha or the monks to his home for a meal. One day, Migara had invited ascetics to his house for a meal, and he wanted Vishakha to serve them food. However, Vishakha refused to feed or serve them food.

Shortly afterward, an old Buddhist monk came to their house asking for alms and was standing outside the house, waiting for alms. Migara, who was eating at the time, saw the monk but completely ignored him without offering him food. Then Vishakha went to the old monk and said to him, "Respected Bhante, my father-in-law is eating stale food." When Migara heard this, he became angry and decided to throw Vishakha out of his house.

But, at her request, the case was referred to arbitrators nominated by his father to investigate several allegations made against her by her father-in-law. Vishakha told Migara that she said this because her father-in-law Migara was taking his food, ignoring the old Buddhist monk standing at the door for alms. Migara had no intention of donating food to satisfy the hunger of the old Buddhist monk. This means his father-in-law was not creating any merit for the future, which is like eating stale food. She said, she did not intend to insult her father-in-law through her statement and she did not consider herself guilty. After her explanation, her father-in-law Migara apologized. However, Vishakha set a condition that her father-in-law Migara would invite the Buddha and his group of monks to his home for Dhamma discourse and for food.

However, he did not agree to this due to the influence of Jain monks. Vishakha then threatened to leave Migara's house and go back to her parents. Migara apologized to her and agreed to invite the Buddha and the Bhikkhu Sangha to his home for religious sermons. When the Buddha and the monks were invited to his home for a meal, Migara refused to donate food to the Buddha or participate in the sermon. After the meal, Vishakha sent him a second message to attend the Buddha's sermon, and he agreed to sit behind the curtain to listen to the Dhamma discourse as advised by his guru, the Jain ascetic. However, when he heard the Buddha's sermon and was influenced by the Buddha's teachings, both Migara and his wife understood the teachings of the Buddha and accepted the Buddha Dhamma. He thus reached the Sotapanna stage, the first stage of spiritual enlightenment.

Donation of Pubbarama Vihar to the Sangha

One day, Vishakha went to the Jetavana Monastry to listen to the dhamma discourse by the Buddha. While entering the monastery, she took off her precious jewelry and gave it to her maid to keep. After the sermon, they left the monastery, but the maid forgot to take the box of jewelry. Venerable Ananda, the Buddha's chief attendant, had the habit of walking around the monastery at the end of each day. Ananda found the jewelry box lying in the monastery and identified it as belonging to Vishakha. After discussing it with the Buddha, he kept it in a safe place. The next day, when Vishakha came for the listening of the discourse, the box of jewelry was returned to her. However, she refused to accept it, stating that since it had been left in the monastery, it now belonged only to the monastery. She felt that it was not right to take back something that had been left in the monastery and was taken care of by the monks. When the monks told her that it was of no use to them, Vishakha decided to sell it.

That jewelry was precious and costly. Therefore, no one in Shravasti was wealthy enough to dare to buy it. Therefore, Vishakha decided to buy it herself and use the money to build a monastery on the eastern side of the Jetavana Monastery. Under the guidance of Maha Moggallana, Visakha spent the money on building the monastery. The monastery was completed in nine months and then donated to the Buddha and his Sangha.

The new monastery had a massive two-story mansion, with each floor comprising five hundred separate halls. The monastery's spire was made of gold and was so large that sixty water pots could be stored inside it. The monastery was known as Pubbarama or Purvarama or Migara Mata Prasada, which means the palace of Migara Mata.

Vishakha invited the Buddha and the Bhikkhu Sangha to stay in the newly built monastery during the four-month rainy season. On the arrival of the Buddha, she donated the Pubbarama Monastery to him. When the dedication ceremony was still going on, Vishakha felt so happy that she started singing songs of joy around the Pubbarama Vihara along with her children and grandchildren.

The Pubbarama Monastery in Shravasti was the largest and most generous donation to the Buddha and his Bhikkhu Sangha. According to Pali literature, the Buddha delivered several important sermons while residing at the Pubbarama Monastery. It is believed that in Shravasti, the Buddha was staying at the Jetavana Monastery and the Pubbarama Monastery each day or night.

Vishakha Became the Mother of Migara

After accepting the Buddha's order, Migara and his wife took refuge in the Buddha, the Dhamma, and the Sangha and became disciples of the Buddha. Migara was always grateful to his daughter-in-law Vishakha for helping him abandon his blind faith in other religious sects and become a disciple of the Buddha. It is recorded in the literature that on the day Visakha donated the Pubbarama Monastery built at Shravasti to the Bhikkhu Sangha, her father-in-law and mother-in-law witnessed Vishakha's devotion and happiness as well as devotion to the Buddha and his Sangha. Migara's gratitude towards Vishakha grew extremely strong, and he requested that she consider him as her son from that point onward. Since then, Vishakha came to be known as 'Migara Mata' (Mother of Migara, her father in law).

Vishakha: The Chief Disciple of Buddha

Vishakha also played an important role in encouraging large numbers of lay women to learn and practice the Buddha's doctrine. Because of her devotion, dedication, and generosity towards the Buddha, his Dhamma, and Sangha, Vishakha was declared the chief female disciple by the Buddha.

As the chief female disciple, Vishakha played a very important role in helping and supporting the Buddha, monks, and nuns whenever there were problems regarding the lay disciples. She visited the Buddha daily, and after listening to the Buddha's teachings, she would wander around the monastery, tending to the needs of the resident monks and bhikkhunis. The Buddha sought her help on several occasions in resolving disciplinary issues that arose among Buddhist nuns. She received permission from the Buddha to look after the monks coming to Shravasti from other regions. It is said that every day, five hundred monks used to come to her house for food, and if she was out of the house, she would hand over the responsibility of feeding the visiting monks to her granddaughter. She fulfilled her role as the Buddha's chief female disciple and chief benefactor by supporting the Buddha and the Sangha as well as common Buddhist disciples. Due to her benevolence, Vishakha had earned so much respect that the people of Shravasti always invited her to their homes on festivals and holidays.

Vishakha's Death

Vishakha had ten sons and ten daughters, and it is said that each of them had an equal number of sons and daughters. However, she retained her beauty and charm until the last days of her life. It is recorded in Buddhist literature that Vishakha died at the age of one hundred and twenty. Spiritually, Vishakha had attained Sotapanna, the first of the four stages of the Buddhist spiritual path to liberation. She will continue to be recognized and remembered in history as one of the foremost Buddhist disciples of the Lord Buddha and his teachings to lift humanity from suffering.

Life of Vishakha offers many profound life lessons through her devotion and her actions in the Buddha's Sangha. Vishakha was known for her extraordinary generosity. She provided food, clothing and support for monks and nuns and built monasteries. She understood the importance of giving without attachment, which is a core Buddhist teaching. Her generosity went beyond material offerings, as she also gave her time, effort and care to others. True wealth lies in generosity and selflessness. By helping others, we cultivate inner joy and peace, transcending material attachments. Dedication to spiritual practice and inner growth is essential for leading a meaningful life.

She proved that one could live in the world, manage family duties, and still follow the path of Dharma. She played an important role in supporting the establishment of the Bhikkhuni Sangha (order of nuns). Her life is a testament to the role women can play in spiritual leadership and community development. Spiritual awakening is accessible to everyone, regardless of gender or social status. Vishakha's life reflects the importance of inclusivity and equality on the spiritual path.

Vishakha's life as a disciple of the Buddha teaches us that the true essence of a fulfilled life lies in generosity, wisdom, and compassion. By integrating spiritual principles with daily responsibilities, she became a model for leading a balanced, mindful, and meaningful life.

4. IMPORTANT EVENTS IN SHRAVASTI

1. Untouchable Sunit became a monk

After the rainy season in Shravasti, the Buddha and the Bhikkhus started a journey to make more and more people aware of the teachings of the Dhamma in the surrounding areas. One day, when the Buddha and the Bhikkhus were going to a village on the banks of the Ganga to beg for alms, the Buddha saw a person carrying feces and urine, whose name was Sunit. His clothes were very dirty and smelled of feces and urine. He moved away from the path of the Buddha and moved towards the banks of the Ganga. Buddha understood this and took the initiative to teach the Dhamma to Sunit. When Sunit changed his path, the Buddha also moved in the same direction. Understanding the Buddha's wish, Sariputta and Meghiya Bhikkhu also followed him. Other Bhikkhus also stopped walking and stayed there.

When Sunit saw that the Buddha was approaching him, he got scared. He put the buckets of filth aside and tried to hide himself, but unable to understand anything, he entered the river in knee-deep water and stood with folded hands. Sunit had left the path so that the Buddha and the Bhikkhu Sangha would not become impure. He knew that he was considered untouchable by social beliefs. Defiling them would be an unpardonable crime. He hoped that after entering the river, the Buddha would go on his way. But the Buddha went to the water's edge and said, "Friend, come near me, so that we can talk to each other."

Sunit folded his hands and said, "Lord, how can I dare to do this."

Why not? Buddha asked.

"I am an untouchable and do not wish to defile you and the Bhikkhus."

The Buddha replied,

"There is no discrimination on the Sadhamma path. You are also a man like us. We are not afraid of being impure."

What is your name?

"Prabhu, my name is Sunit."

"Sunit, would you like to become a Bhikkhu?"

"Lord, I cannot become a Bhikkhu because, according to the prevailing social system, I come from the untouchable class."

"Sunit, I have already told you that there is no place for caste on the path of enlightenment. Just as the rivers Ganga, Yamuna, Rohini lose their separate existence when they meet the sea, similarly the person who leaves his home and adopts the path of the Sadhamma, one leaves one's birth caste, no matter how noble or lowly one is born in. Sunit, if you wish, you too can become a Bhikkhu like the rest."

Sunit could not believe his ears, so he placed his joined hands on his forehead and said,

"Lord, no one has ever spoken to me so kindly. If you accept me as your disciple, I will follow the teachings."

The Buddha handed over his alms bowl to Bhante Meghiya and came forward and held Sunit's hand, and said to Sariputta,

"Sariputta, please help Sunit to bath in the water. We will offer Sunit's pravajya on the banks of the river itself."

Bhante Sariputta smiled, placed his alms bowl on the ground, and proceeded to help the Buddha. Bhante Sariputta and the Buddha bathed Sunita in the river. The Buddha asked Bhante Meghiya and Bhante Anand to bring the civara.

Buddha admitted the untouchable Sunit into the Bhikkhu Sangha. Sunit was taken to Jetavana. After Sunit's Pravajya, arrangements were made for him to receive education under the supervision of Bhante Sariputta.

There was an uproar among the upper castes in the capital Shravasti. Never before in the history of Kosala had any untouchable been accepted into the spiritual community. Many condemned the Buddha for violating sacred tradition. A group of religious leaders met King Prasenjit and expressed their deep dissatisfaction over Sunit's conversion to Buddha's Sangh. King Prasenjit promised the leaders that he would look into the matter.

King Prasenjit approached the Buddha and, after proper greetings, he sat beside the Buddha and explained about the dissatisfaction of the religious groups regarding Sunit's entry into the Bhikkhu Sangha. Responding to the public's accusations and King Prasenjit's concerns over Sunit's inclusion in the Sangh, the Buddha said,

"Accepting the untouchables into the Sangha was only a matter of time. Our method is to promote equality and we do not recognize castes. Although we may face difficulties during Sunit's consecration, the first of its kind in history, future generations will thank us for it. We must have courage. Your Excellency, in the eyes of the wise on the path to liberation, there is no caste and all people are equal. Every human being's blood is red and every human being's tears are salty. We are all human beings. We have to find a way to enable people to realize their full dignity and potential. That is why I welcome Sunit in the Bhikkhu Sangha."

Expressing his gratitude, King Prasenjit said, "Now I understand. I also know that the path you have chosen is full of obstacles and difficulties, but I know that you have the strength and courage to overcome all such obstacles. I will do everything in my power to support the true teaching."

The incidence of Sunit's conversion highlights Buddhism's message of spiritual equality. Despite being born into a low caste, performing menial tasks such as sweeping streets and scavenging, Sunit was accepted by the Buddha with no regard of his social status. The Buddha's act of embracing Sunit as a monk challenged the rigid caste system and the belief that one's worth was defined by birth. Every human being has the potential for spiritual growth, liberation and true worth comes from one's actions, wisdom and mindfulness, not from birth or social status. The Buddha saw beyond societal labels and focused on Ssunit's inherent potential as a human being. Compassion is the heart of Buddhism. One should extend kindness and understanding to all, especially to those marginalized by society. Sunit lived a life of oppression and poverty, trapped by the social norms of the caste system. After his ordination, Sunit achieved enlightenment, illustrating that the path of Dhamma allows one to transcend not only internal suffering but also external social constraints. Through the practice of mindfulness, ethical conduct and wisdom, Sunit was able to free from the limitations imposed by his caste to attain spiritual freedom. The Buddha's teachings provide a path to inner freedom and peace for all people, regardless of their circumstances.

2.Two Important Decisions in Shravasti

Two important decisions were made at the Dhamma Conference held in the Vishakha Hall of Shravasti. The first was that Ananda would become the Buddha's permanent attendant, and the second was that the Buddha would spend every rainy season in Shravasti. This was the twentieth rainy retreat of the Buddha after his enlightenment.

The first proposal was made by Bhante Sariputta, who said that Ananda had the best memory among them and could remember every word spoken by the Buddha. In this way, Ananda will be able to remember whatever was said in any Dhamma Desana or during a conversation with any seeker. In this way, they should preserve the words of the Buddha. Due to their carelessness, they had lost many words uttered by the Buddha. They urged him to take up the responsible task of being the Buddha's assistant for the sake of all of them and for future generations.

All the monks accepted Sariputta's proposal, but Ananda showed hesitation and said,

"I see many problems in this proposal. The first issue is whether the Buddha would even want to keep me as his assistant. The Buddha was cautious about not giving special recognition to members of the Shakya dynasty. He is even harsh towards his mother, Bhikkhuni Mahaprajapati, and maintained a distance. He never kept Rahul in his hut nor did he eat with him. I am afraid, If I am chosen to be his assistant, some bhikkhus may accuse me of being a favorite of the Buddha. If I try to correct someone's faults, they can accuse me of taking the Buddha's side."

Ananda looked at Sariputta and said,

"Buddha respects Sariputta very much. Sariputta is the person with the greatest talent. Moreover, the Buddha consults Sariputta before making any decision. It would be appropriate for Sariputta to become the Buddha's assistant."

Sariputta laughed and said,

"Ananda, please accept this proposal. If you do not accept this, then it will result in a loss of the Dhamma for this generation and future generations."

Ananda remained silent on this. With great hesitation, he said,

"I can consider the proposal only when the Buddha accepts these requests of mine;

- The Buddha will never give me his robe.
- The Buddha will not give me the food he received as alms.
- Buddha will not ask me to stay in his hut.
- Buddha will not ask me to accompany him while going for alms or to attend to the invitations from disciples.
- If the disciples invite me for food, then even Buddha may join me.
- The people who come to meet Buddha, he will use my discretion regarding meeting them or not.

- Buddha will allow me to ask him again about those things that I have not understood properly.
- The Buddha will tell me again the essence of the Dhamma when I may not be present.

Bhante Upali got up and said,

"Ananda's conditions seem to be quite fair. But I do not agree to his fourth condition. If Ananda does not go along with Buddha when he is invited, then how will we be able to hear and remember the Dhamma discussion that took place there which will be useful for the future generations and for all of us? Whenever a follower invites the Buddha, in addition to Ananda, another Bhikku should also accompany him. In this way, there will not be any allegations that Ananda is being given special favouritism."

Everyone accepted Ananda's words and understood that the problem of finding the best assistant for the Buddha had been resolved.

After this, Sariputta started talking on the second proposal that every year Buddha will come to Shravasti to reside during the rainy season. Because Shravasti is a good place where Jetavana, Purvarama, and the school of bhikkhunis are present, and all other places are in the vicinity. Many people plan to listen to the Buddha's teachings when the Buddha resides in the same place every year during the rainy season. Anathapindika and Mahishi Vishakha have promised to make arrangements for food, medicine, clothing, and stay for all the people coming to Shravasti including the Bhikkhu Sangha, during the rainy season.

The bhikkhus agreed to do so every year. After the conference ended, they went straight to Buddha's hut to present both proposals to him. Buddha happily accepted both proposals.

3.Allegations of murder against Buddha and Sangha

One day, when the Buddha and the monks were leaving the monastery to seek alms in Shravasti, a number of policemen entered the Jetavana to recover the body of a woman. The monks were stunned and could not understand why the police had come to the monastery to find the dead body of a woman. On inquiry by Bhante Bhadiya, it was reported that a member of a large sect of Shravasti named Sundari had been murdered and reported to be buried behind the monastery. The monks said that nothing would be found there, but the police remained adamant on searching. When the search was over, everyone was surprised to see the body of a woman found buried in a shallow grave behind the Buddha's hut. No one could understand how the woman died and who buried her there. The Bhikkhus recognized the body of a beautiful lady who used to visit Jetavana frequently to listen to the religious discourses of the Buddha. When the police took away the body, the Buddha told the monks to go on their alms rounds as usual. He said to keep their posture of alertness intact.

On the same day, people from Sundari's sect took out a procession with her body. They were shouting slogans, saying:

"This is the dead body of Sundari. This dead body has been found from the premises of Jetavana Vihar. But the Buddha disciples of the Sakya dynasty who practice to live a pure life without lust, have raped Sundari and have also tried to hide her dead body. Their words about kindness, compassion and equality are completely false. See with your own eyes."

The citizens of Shravasti were very agitated over this incident. The faith of many devout disciples of the Buddha also started wavering. In fact, it was a deep and well-planned conspiracy to defame the Buddha and the Sangha among the common people and the ordinary disciples of the Buddha.

The religious sects threatened by the Buddha's growing popularity seized the opportunity to openly criticize the Buddha and condemn the Sangha. Whenever the bhikkhus went to the houses for alms, they were asked various unpleasant questions. Sometimes, they were condemned and assaulted by common people. The bhikkhus maintained their gentleness and continued their work by remaining composed in consciousness.

One afternoon, the Buddha called the bhikkhus and addressed them all. He said,

"Unfair accusations can be made anywhere and at any time. You need not feel ashamed. False accusations will spread for a few days and then die down. Tomorrow, when you go for alms and if anyone talks about all this, you say, whoever is responsible for this deed will get its fruits."

The Buddha could instill in them a great courage with these few words. Meanwhile, Mahishi Vishakha, deeply worried by this incident, decided to investigate the matter privately. For this purpose, she went to Anathpindika and discussed this topic in detail. Both of them decided to investigate the whole matter secretly so that the real culprit could be found. He told his plan to Prince Jeta, who also promised to help in this work.

Within seven days, the detectives found the culprits when two persons drank excessively and started fighting among themselves, and one of them revealed the secret behind the killing of Sundari. The police caught all those accused, who confessed to the crime and told that the people of Sundari's sect had given them a good amount of money for killing Sundari and burying her body behind the Buddha's hut at Jetavana.

King Prasenajit immediately went to Jetavanaa to tell the news that the murderers had been caught. The King expressed his unwavering loyalty towards the Sangha and expressed happiness that everyone has become aware of the reality. The Buddha asked the King to forgive all those responsible for this crime. The Buddha said that if people do not overcome their malice and hatred, crimes will continue to happen again and again.

The people of Shravasti then again began looking at the Bhikkhus with great respect and honor.

4. Buddha was falsely accused of sexual misconduct

Once, the Buddha was staying in Shravasti during the rainy season. Some people falsely accused him of committing adultery with a woman and making her pregnant. It was evident that some people in Shravasti were opposed to Buddha's preaching and harbored ill will towards Buddha and his Sangha. Therefore, they planned and convinced a beautiful girl named Chincha to do something malicious to undermine their faith and religion. According to the plan, the girl would go to Jetavana every day wearing a beautiful sari and carrying a bouquet of flowers, pretending she wanted to meet the Buddha and offer flowers. However, she did not attend the Dhamma sermon. When the audience was about to leave the premises, she used to stand deliberately in front of the Dhamma room. In the beginning, when people asked what she was doing there, she used to smile and remained silent. After giving vague answers for a few days, one day she said, "I am going to Bhikkhu Buddha."

Finally, after a few days, she said, "Sleeping in Jetavana is very pleasurable."

This seemed peculiar to people and various apprehensions arose in the minds of the Dhamma seekers and well-wishers, but no one dared to speak up about this issue.

One day, Chincha attended Buddha's Dhamma Desna.

She said,

"Buddha talks a lot about Dhamma and thus, he is respected a lot, but he does not care about this vulnerable lady like me whom Buddha made pregnant. Your child is growing in my womb. Will you take responsibility for it?"

With these words, she began to cry bitterly.

A wave of concern swept through the Sangha. Everyone started looking towards Buddha. The Buddha just smiled calmly and said, "Oh! my sister, only you and I know how true what you are saying is."

Buddha's calm smile staggered Chincha. But she said, "It is absolutely right, only you and I know how true and how false my statement is."

The monks and people of the Sangha suspected that Chincha was lying. Many worshipers were standing in anger and wanted to know the truth behind what she said.

Chincha got scared; she felt that many people were now ready to scold or beat her. When she started running away, she collided with a wooden post. After a strong collision with a standing pillar, she fell to the ground.

When she somehow managed to stand up, a large cloth bundle tied around her stomach fell onto her feet. She screamed and sat there, feeling ashamed. Now, her stomach was completely flat.

The community present there heaved a sigh of relief. Many people started laughing at her, while some began criticizing Chincha. People asked her to leave the monastery.

Buddha continued to preach his Dhamma as if nothing had happened.

5. A Sad story of Bhikkhuni Patachara.

Patachara, as named, was the daughter of a very rich and prestigious family. She was very beautiful and intelligent. Since the social environment for young girls was not good in those days, she was not allowed to go out of her house.

When she was of marriageable age, she fell in love with the servant of her house. When her family learned of her love affair with their servant, they did not approve of the relationship. She wanted to marry him, but her parents did not support her proposal. They wanted to marry her off to some other boy, which she was not in favor of. So, she planned to run away. She eloped with her servant and married him. A few months after the marriage, her first son was born. During her second pregnancy, along with her husband, she decided to go to her parents to give birth to her child. When she was traveling to her ancestral home, a fierce storm suddenly arose, and she went into labour. In the stormy atmosphere of the forest, she delivered a baby. To protect his children and wife from the rain and storm, the husband started collecting branches and dry twigs of some trees. While doing so, he became a victim of a snake bite and died on the spot due to the deadly poison. There was no end to Patachara's sorrow. She was unable to understand anything about the first son and the newborn child or how to proceed. She somehow controlled her terrible sadness and pain. She waited in that dense forest until morning. She took the newborn baby in one hand and the other child in the other hand, and walked to Shravasti, where her parents lived.

Due to torrential rain throughout the night on the way, the river was overflowing at full speed. She decided to cross the river, so she placed the newborn child on the river bank and took the elder child to the other bank of the river and asked him to wait. She returned and placed her newborn child on her head and started crossing the river. When she was in the middle of the river, an eagle picked up her child and took it into the sky. She started crying to save her child. The eldest boy on the other side felt that his mother was calling him. He jumped into the river to reach his mother and got absorbed in the flow of the river.

At last, Patachara reached the other shore and became unconscious due to her extreme sorrow. After regaining consciousness, she got up and started walking towards Shravasti. One more tragic event was added to her sorrow as her parents' house had collapsed and been destroyed due to the strong storm and rain and her parents had died under the debris. The day she reached Shravasti, the cremation of her parents was taking place.

Seeing and hearing all these unfortunate events, Patachara became unconscious right there on the road. Now she did not want to live. It is also said that due to the sequence of such tragic events, she became distraught and threw her garments, starting to walk naked on the road. Some people took pity on her condition, covered her with garments, and took her to Jetavana.

The Buddha listened to her sad story and said,

"Patachara, you have suffered a lot. But life is not all about suffering and misfortune. Be courageous and practice the path of Saddhamma. One day you will be able to laugh even at your terrible suffering. You will know that despite sorrow, life can be lived with peace and happiness."

Patachara bowed before the Buddha and requested that he grant her Pravajya. Then the Buddha left her under the care and protection of the bhikkhuni Mahaprajapati Gautami. Mahaprajapati Gautami and the other bhikkhunis loved her very much, helping her to overcome her sorrow.

One day, while washing her feet, she noticed the water being absorbed into the earth and drying up. Then suddenly she became aware of the impermanence of the elements. For many days and nights, she practiced Dhamma with devotion and was able to understand the Buddha's teachings. Later, Patachara was counted among the Buddha's principal disciples.

6. Utpalavarna became Bhikkhuni

Utpalavarna was a Buddhist bhikkhuni who was considered one of the Buddha's disciples. Her complexion was as bright as a blue lotus, hence she was named 'Utpalavarna,' which means 'the color of a blue lotus flower'.

According to the Pali tradition, Utpalavarna was born as the daughter of the treasurer of Shravasti. In addition to her physical beauty, her intelligence also started shining day by day. She was a topic of discussion and attraction among the youth of that time. Due to her beauty, proposals started coming from many prestigious sons and princes seeking her hand in marriage. All of whom were more glorious, powerful and prosperous.

Princes sent fabulous gifts to win her heart, imagining her presence in their palaces as a wife. It was beyond the power of her parents to make everyone happy. If the beautiful Utpalavarna had been married to one person, everyone else would have been angry and would have harmed her parents. In such a difficult situation, Utpalvarna's father became very worried. Seeing her father worried, the beautiful Utpalavarna said – "Father, why are you sad?"

Her father, hiding his heartfelt pain, replied,

"Oh, my daughter, many princes and noble sons want to make you their wife, but how can I satisfy everyone? If I marry you to one person, then everyone else will fight."

Before he could say anything further, his throat got choked.

Her noble father was torn between rival clans, struggling with the dilemma of social expectations. Nevertheless, he recognized the strength of his daughter's conviction and thus suggested that she should give up the worldly life and accept the ascetic life. He urged her to give up the momentary pleasures of the world.

She considered all circumstances and thought over the advice of her father, Utpalavarna entered the Bhikkhuni Snagha (nunnery) with the blessings of her parents. Rapidly, she climbed the spiritual ladder, transcending worldly attachments to attain the revered status of a great arhat bhikkhuni.

In some literature, there is mention of another side to the story of her conversion to Buddhism. Before converting to Buddhism and becoming a bhikkhuni, Utpalavarna had a tumultuous life as a wife and prostitute. Utpalvarna was born the daughter of a merchant and was married to a local man. Her father-in-law had died, and Utpalvarna later learned that her mother-in-law had established illicit relations with her son. She felt very bad about this strange relationship and went away from home sadly, leaving her newborn daughter behind. Later on, Utpalavarna married another man. Married life continued well for a few years. Her husband suddenly considered a second marriage. She came to know that her husband's second wife was none other than her daughter from her first husband. Fed up with the reality of such events in life, she left her second husband's house as well.

Her pain and suffering were so bitter that she started hating the whole world and neither loved nor trusted anyone in the world. She became a dancer and started earning herself diamonds, money and all material comforts.

Fed up with lust and deceit in real life, she took refuge in the Buddha and was tonsured to become a Bhikkhuni under the guidance of Maha Maudgalayan (Pali: Moggallan).

Maudgalayan said,

"Why are you so pessimistic? No matter how bad your past was, you can still make changes and have the power to create a better future. Even dirty clothes can be washed. With a heart full of confusion and worries, one can be liberated through self-awareness and become purified. The teaching of the Buddha is that every one of us must be able to attain peace and happiness."

Utpalavarna said,

"My life is full of sinful deeds. I'm afraid even Buddha wouldn't be able to help me."

Utpalvarna covered her face and began crying. Maudgalayan allowed her to cry for as long as possible so that she could empty herself emotionally. After she started crying, Maudgalayan began telling her about Saddhamma. He took her to the Buddha. The Buddha inquired about her in a compassionate tone and asked if she was willing to receive Saddhamma teachings from Bhikkhuni Mahaprajapati. She was accepted into the Buddha's Sangha, and after strictly following the Dhamma for four years, she was able to take her honorable place in the Sangha.

After becoming a Bhikkhuni, she was living alone in the forest. In a cruel twist of fate, Nanda, a misguided man from her past, attacks her hut located in the forest due to an old enmity. Utpalavarna faced the sexual assault calmly and without fear, her mind untouched by turmoil. After the incident, when the Buddha was asked for his opinion on the incident, the Buddha said that Utpalavarna did not break the monastic rule of chastity because she had not given any consent. Due to this incident, a rule was made to prevent such incidents under which bhikkhunis were prohibited from living alone in the forest.

Undeterred by the shadows of the past, Utpalavarna continued her spiritual journey, facing the temptations and evils of life with determination. She mastered psychic powers, leading the Buddha to declare her the foremost in psychic power among his female disciples. The Buddha also praised Utpalavarna for her teaching and leadership abilities. Utpalavarna and Khema share the title of chief disciples with their male counterparts Maha Maudgalayana and Sariputta.

The story of Utpalavarna resonates as an indomitable spirit overcoming adversity, exemplifying that an immaculate mind, fortified by the Buddha's teachings, remains impervious to the injustices of the world.

7. Story of Kisa Gautami

Once, the Buddha was living in Jetavana in Shravasti. At that time, Kisa Gautami, the wife of a wealthy man in Shravasti brought the dead body of her son to the Buddha in the hope that the Buddha would revive him. The story goes like this.

Gautami was so thin that people began to call her 'Kisa Gautami' which means 'Skinny Gautami'. Kisa Gautami married a wealthy man. When her only son was one year old, he fell ill and died suddenly. Kisa Gautami could not bear the death of her only son. When she did not succeed in reviving him herself, Kisa Gautami asked her relatives for help. They could see that the child was dead. In her pain and grief, she was unable to see or understand that her son was dead. She walked down the street with her son's body in her arms, going from house to house asking if anyone had a medicine that would cure her son. It was clear to everyone she asked that the child could not be cured with the help of medicines, and poor Kisa Gautami was so distraught that she was unable to accept the fact of her child's death. They tried to help her as best they could, gently telling her that medicines would not help, and that she would have to accept that the boy was dead and take him to the cemetery for burial. But Kisa Gautami's grief and anguish were so deep that she was unable to understand what the people of the town were saying to her. While seeking help, she arrived at the home of an elderly person in the city. The elder was a very wise person. He thought this child was clearly beyond the help of medicine, but the mother was in great need of help. No doctor could help the child, but there was a great doctor nearby who would know how to help this desperate woman. The elder said to Kisa Gautami,

"Good woman, go to the Buddha who is the Enlightened One, and ask him if he has any medicine for your son."

When Kisa Gautami heard about the Buddha, she asked where the Buddha might be and hurried there, carrying the lifeless body of her dead son in her arms. When she reached the place where the Buddha was staying, she went straight to the Buddha and fell at his feet, and said to him crying,

"Lord Buddha, I beg you, please give me the medicine I need to awaken my child from his sleep."

The Buddha immediately understood Kisa Gautami's situation and state of mind and said to her,

"Good lady, I have some medicine for you, but for this medicine to work you have to bring a small amount of mustard seeds from a house in the city."

She said,

"Yes, Tathagat, I can certainly do that,"

Mustard seeds were one of the cheapest spices, and she knew that almost every house in the city would have mustard seeds.

But the Buddha put a condition before her.

He said,

"You have to bring these mustard seeds from a house in the city where no one has died, and where no one has ever lost a loved one."

Kisa Gautami did not understand what difference this would make, but she accepted the Buddha's instruction and hurried off to get mustard seeds, thinking they would cure her child.

Confidently, she knocked on the first door she came across and asked if they could give her a small quantity of mustard seeds. The people in the house could see the state Kisa Gautami was in, still holding her son's body, and they gave her the mustard seeds she wanted. As she turned triumphantly to return to the Buddha, she suddenly remembered the second part of the Buddha's instructions and turning to the owner of the house, asked,

"By the way, has anyone ever died in this house or have any of you ever lost a loved one?"

"Yes, of course," came the answer, "our grandmother died a few weeks ago."

Kisa Gautami was disappointed and gave the mustard seeds back, but went on to the next house, thinking she had been unlucky at the first house. Again, the people in the house had some mustard seeds, but again someone had died in the house, so she went to the next house. The same thing happened in the next house. Kisa Gautami was not going to give up in her tremendous grief and kept going from house to house, asking the same question. In one house, the father had died; in another, the daughter; and in the third, the husband. After a while, Kisa Gautami stopped asking even for mustard seeds because she could not find any house in which a family member had not died. Finally, by the evening, she realized that in every family she went, someone had died. There was no house free from death.

Eventually, she came to understand what the Buddha wanted her to discover for herself – that suffering is a part of life and death comes to all of us. Kisa Gautami's mind began to realize that she was not alone or unusual in losing her child. She realized that the universe was not troubling her and was not singling her out for any special punishment.

She was just one of many grieving parents. Kisa Gautami accepted her son's death and took him on his final journey to the cemetery.

After burying her son, Kisa Gautami calmly walked back through the streets to where the Buddha was staying. Kisa Gautami went up to him, bowed respectfully before him, and thanked him for his teaching. The Buddha asked her if she had managed to bring the mustard seeds, and she replied,

"No, Lord Buddha, I did not. It is easy to get mustard seeds, but it is equally difficult to find a home untouched by death."

"Oh, wise woman," said the Buddha, "When I said that I had some medicine for you, you must have thought that I was promising to cure your son. But in fact, the medicine was not for your son, but for you. I can see that the medicine has done its work, and now you see clearly that birth and death cannot be avoided and are part of the reality of existence for each person and all living beings."

The Buddha then recited this verse in Pali which means:

"People are heavily burdened with so many worries;

They are driven by worries about children, money, property, and reputation.

No matter how much they are attached to life, death comes to everyone.

Sweeping away everything like a great flood sweeps away a sleeping village."

Hearing this verse and influenced by the day's events, Kisa Gautami prayed to the Buddha to accept her in the Bhikkhuni Sangha.

Many years later, one evening as she was watching the flickering of the oil lamp flame in her monastery, she noticed how easily the flame could be extinguished by a slight breeze, and she came to a deep understanding of the fragile and temporary nature of life.

One day she came to the Buddha and after appropriate greetings, she sat down on one side.

The Buddha recited this verse in Pali, comparing a life of delusion and ignorance to a life of right understanding, which means:

"A person may live a hundred years,

who has not understood the nature of reality.

But a single day of life is far more valuable to a person.

who has understood the nature of reality."

Gautami took the Buddha's teachings to heart and replied.

"Lord Buddha, thank you for your great compassion. The Buddha said, "A single day of understanding is better than a hundred years of ignorance."

The Buddha praised Gautami's understanding. Even today, she is considered one of the most prominent disciples of the Buddha.

The story of Kisa Gotami is usually told to remind us of impermanence. Sorrow, sadness, happiness, and love are always going to be a part of our lives. We need to remember to practice so we are able to guide our lives and not be led by these passing emotions.

8. Death of Devadatta in Jetavan

Devadutta was the son of Suddhodana's sister, Pamita. When the Buddha visited Kapilavastu and preached among the Sakya princes, many Sakya princes joined the Buddha's Sangha. This was the time when Devadutta also joined the Sangha.

It is said that there was some personal rivalry between Devadatta and Siddhartha since their childhood. This can be understood well from a childhood story. Once, Siddhartha was roaming the country with his cousin Devadatta, who had a bow and arrows. Devadatta attacked the flying swan with his arrow, and the swan fell to the ground in pain. Both the boys ran forward to pick him up, but Siddhartha reached there first and holding it gently, took out the arrow from its feathers, applied some cool leaves to the wound so that it would not bleed and patted it with his gentle hand, bringing the frightened bird back to life. But seeing his cousin caressing the swan, Devadatta became very angry and requested Siddhartha to hand over the injured bird to him as he had shot it with his arrow. However, Siddhartha refused to give it to him, stating that if the bird had died, it would have belonged to Devadatta. Since the bird was alive and not dead, it belonged to

Siddhartha, the one who had actually taken possession of it, and therefore he wanted to keep it for himself. But still, Devadatta did not relent in his demand.

Siddhartha proposed to take this dispute to the council for a decision. Devadatta agreed that his dispute should be referred to a full council of wise people in the country for settlement. Accordingly, the Council was convened, and the question was presented before them. In the council, some argued one way, while the rest argued the other way. Some said that the bird should belong to Devadatta, while others said that Siddhartha was right in keeping it with him. But at last, a man in the meeting whom no one had ever seen before stood up and said,

"Life belongs to him who tries to save it; life cannot belong to one who only wants to destroy it. Therefore, the swan should be given to Siddhartha."

All the others in the Council instantly agreed with these wise words and allowed Prince Siddhartha to keep the swan whose life he had thus saved. Siddhartha looked after the swan tenderly until its wound healed. He fed the bird and let it fly into the open air.

It has been extensively described in many texts that as a young prince, Siddhartha had always been everyone's favorite. He was obedient, kind, and considerate. He also mastered every skill and sport. Devadutta was always jealous of him. Everyone liked Siddhartha. Why was he always chosen as the best? Why don't people see some great things in me? Devadutta used to question himself, as his narrow mind could not understand that it was his own arrogance, cruel nature, and thoughtlessness that had driven people away from him.

When Siddhartha transcended into the Buddha, Devadutta saw the Sakya princes adopting his doctrine of Dhamma. He also decided to give up his life as a prince and follow the teachings of the Buddha. He entered into union with Ananda and Aniruddha. For some time, his jealousy and hatred were suppressed as he learned new knowledge through the Buddha with great passion and labor. Within a short time, he developed his mind rapidly through meditation and reached the first stage of knowledge. Seeing his efforts and progress, Sariputta praised his hard work.

However, this was only a temporary relief. His old hidden anger and jealousy towards the Buddha came back into his dark heart. Seeing the popularity and respect of Buddha among the common people, kings, rich and poor, he became filled with hatred and jealousy and started plotting against Buddha and the Sangha.

In his early days, he was a good monk known for his loving kindness and psychic powers. Later, he became proud of worldly gains and fame. As his ill will and jealousy towards the Buddha increased, he became the Buddha's greatest personal enemy.

Then, one day, when the Buddha was sitting in the midst of a large gathering, preaching to the king and the people, Devadutta stood up and covered his right shoulder with his upper garment as a sign of respect, and he folded his hands in respect for the Buddha. Devadatta stood and said,

"Glorious Buddha, you are now old, quite advanced in age and on the threshold of the last stage of your life. Respected Lord! Let the noble Buddha now live in peace without worrying about anything. He should hand over the Sangha to me. I will lead and take care of the Sangha."

Buddha said:

"Devadatta, this is not right. You should not aspire to take care of and lead the Sangha."

Devadatta made the same request a second time, and the Buddha rejected it. When Devadatta made the request for the third time, the Buddha said:

"Devadatta, I will not hand over the charge of the Sangha even to senior monks like Sariputta and Maha Maudgalayana. Therefore, the question of handing over the administration of the Sangha to a person like you does not arise."

The Buddha rejected this request once and for all. Devadatta became angry at the Buddha's words. He felt humiliated in front of the king and many disciples. Devadutta became angry and unhappy over the Buddha's reply. After paying obeisance to the Buddha, he departed. As a result, Devadatta became very angry and thus decided to take revenge on the Buddha.

One of the most powerful patrons of the Buddha and his Sangha was the Magadha King Bimbisara, who remained on the throne for fifty-two years and had known Siddhartha very well before he became the Buddha. Devadutta decided to seek help from Ajatashatru, the son of King Bimbisara. Devadatta thought that if the Magadha King Bimbisara was removed, the royal patronage and support received by the Buddha would stop, resulting in the weakening of the Buddha and the Sangha.

Devadutta shared this wicked plan with Ajatashatru to seize power from his father, King Bimbisara. It was decided that the prince would take control of the kingdom, while Devadatta would take over the Buddha's Sangha, and the new king would become the guardian of the new spiritual leader, Devadatta.

Accordingly, Bimbisara was imprisoned and his son assumed power. Because he understood the Buddha's teachings about impermanence, King Bimbisara was not fazed by being thrown into prison. He also flourished there. He took his imprisonment as an opportunity to meditate and live a life of simplicity. Due to this, he became more satisfied with his new life. Ultimately, Ajatshatru ordered Bimbisara to be tortured, resulting in Bimbisara's death. However, Devdutt did not receive the royal patronage to the Sangha. Thus, his wicked plan failed.

When the Buddha turned 72 years old, Devadatta began to exhibit a lack of good character that could no longer be ignored. According to known sources, the Buddha had by this time become a renowned Dhamma preacher. Since he began preaching the Dhamma to common people, kings, and the poor, the Buddha had attracted many prominent monks as well as wealthy merchants and renowned royal patrons to his teachings. As his fame grew, so did the comforts of the Sangha. Monks who once wore robes made from discarded cloth were now being provided with robes made from new cloth. The monks who once went from door to door begging for food were now being invited to dine with kings and merchants. Monks who once lived in temporary huts outside the villages were now residing in permanent buildings within the monastery complex. This change in the Sangha's lifestyle became the subject of Devadatta's jealousy and hatred against the Buddha.

Then Devadatta tried to make another move to weaken the Buddha's Sangha and its disciples. Accordingly, one day he tried a fraudulent plan involving 500 monks so that he could divide the Sangha community. During the dhamma desana, he proposed a list of some additional rules that should be made mandatory for all monks. These rules were:

- All monks should live in the forest.
- All monks should live solely on the alms received from households.
- All monks must wear attire made from discarded clothing and must not accept any attire from lay people.
- All monks should live under trees.
- All monks should avoid eating fish or meat.

The Buddha replied that those who wished to follow the first four precepts could follow them and he refused to make them mandatory except for the fifth rule. Devadatta used this opportunity to mislead 500 monks and became their leader. Later, on the Buddha's request, Sariputta and Maha Maudgalayana went to Devadatta, taught the misguided monks about the true meaning of the Dhamma. After hearing the true meaning of Dhamma from the chief disciple of Lord Buddha, 500 monks returned back to Lord Buddha's fold.

Devadatta then planned to kill the Buddha and also to weaken the Buddha's Sangha. For the first time, Devadutta employed swordsmen to assassinate the Buddha. While attempting to kill the Buddha, they saw him sitting in meditation under a moonlit night, very serene, quiet, and compassionate; they also became compassionate towards the Buddha and they abandoned their plan to kill him. Instead, they all knelt before Buddha and confessed their crime.

Then, in despair, Devadatta himself tried to kill the Buddha. Once when the Buddha was walking down Giddakuti mountain, Devadatta climbed the mountain peak and threw a large stone at the Buddha. While passing down, the stone collided with another large stone, leading to many pieces that reduced its velocity considerably, and only a small piece of the stone hurt the Buddha's foot. The Buddha, therefore, was harmless.

After Devadatta failed in his first two attempts to kill the Buddha, he hatched another plan to kill him. This time, Devadatta convinced the royal elephant keeper to release an elephant named Nalagiri, forcing it to drink toddy (wine made from palm trees) and releasing it on the path of the Buddha. The ferocious and now intoxicated animal walked on the streets. People ran away after seeing it. Nevertheless, the Buddha continued walking in his usual dignity and restraint, although Ānanda tried to stop and protect him. Meanwhile, a frightened woman could not pick up the child from the road while saving herself from the fierce elephant. When the advancing animal was about to crush the child, the Buddha in his usual posture touched the elephant's forehead and caressed it gently. After the Buddha patted the elephant, it calmed down and sat down on its knees in front of the Lord Buddha. People saw that the Buddha preached Dhamma to the elephant.

However, the Nalagiri elephant incident made Devadatta very unpopular, and therefore, he had to flee from the city. Furthermore, to respect public opinion, the King withdrew all the royal favors he had received up to that point.

Devadatta made many conspiracies and attempts to kill the Buddha and harm his Sangha, yet the Buddha showed no hatred or ill will towards Devadatta.

Once, Devadatta fell ill and realized that what he had done towards the Buddha was wrong. He realized this when his death was approaching.

Devadatta felt remorse and regretted his actions. He contemplated the impermanence of life at the end of his life. A pang of fear appeared in his heart. He repented, wondering why he had not paid attention to the teachings of the Dhamma when he had the opportunity. How had he strayed so far from the truth? Staggering on his feet, he decided to approach the Buddha to ask for forgiveness for his serious mistakes.

Devadatta's death in Shravasti

Devadatta had been suffering from an illness for a long time, which had made him so weak that he could not even walk. His condition continued to deteriorate for several months. He decided to go to the Buddha's place and apologize for his actions, but it was too late. Finally, when he realized that he was about to die, he sent a message to the Buddha requesting to be allowed to see him one last time. Devadatta thought that the Buddha would definitely see him and forgive him for his misdeeds. He had arranged for some people to carry him on a stretcher to Jetavana in Shravasti, where the Buddha was staying at that time. While on his way to see the Buddha, he became seriously ill near the gate of the Jetavana Monastery and died before he could see the Lord Buddha. But before dying, he took refuge in the Buddha, his Dhamma, and the Sangha.

Lesson we can learn from Devadatta's life

Devadatta's story serves as an example of ambition, jealousy and the consequences of negative actions. Ambition without humility can lead to downfall. In the spiritual path, ego is a major obstacle that can destroy the very progress one is trying to make. This demonstrates the law of karma: negative actions bring negative results. The law of cause and effect is a central principle in Buddhism, reminding us that every action has consequences. This highlights the importance of maintaining compassion even toward those who act as enemies. Compassion is the antidote to hatred and jealousy. Pride in one's attainments can lead to delusion and downfall. His story serves as a cautionary words about the challenges on the spiritual path and the importance of inner purification.

5. DHAMMA SERMONS GIVEN BY BUDDHA IN SHRAVASTI

I. To the General Public

1. We should protect the lives of all living beings

One day when the Buddha and some monks were on their way to Shravasti to seek alms, they saw children catching crabs in a rice field. Children were catching crabs, cutting off their claws and releasing them back into the rice field. Everyone was clapping happily. In this way, they kept catching crabs one after the other.

When the children saw the Buddha and the monks coming, they saluted them and got ready to catch crabs again. The Buddha felt very sad at what the children were doing.

Buddha forbade the children from doing so and said, "Children, if someone cuts off your limbs, will you feel pain or not?"

The children's answer was: "Yes, Gurudev."

"Did you know that even crabs want to live like you?"

The children remained silent. The Buddha continued his statement.

"The crab is also a father like your father, the crab is someone's brother, sister, mother and son."

Seeing this, the villagers also gathered to watch the conversation between Buddha and the children.

Buddha said to the villagers and children,

"Every living creature has the right to enjoy a sense of security and well-being. We must protect life and give happiness to all creatures, whether small or big, two-legged or four-legged, swimming in water, flying or creeping; they all have the right to live, just as we love our own lives, and we should not harm other living beings. We should do everything to save life. We must protect the lives of all living beings."

Buddha further said,

"Just as a mother protects her child by risking her life, we should generously protect every living being. Be it day or night, while standing or walking, sitting or sleeping, we should always keep this feeling in our heart."

Buddha said,

"Children, release the crab you are holding."

Then he said to each person,

"Thus, only one who practices love in life enjoys their life and sleeps well and wakes up happily. Yes, there are no nightmares at night, you have no sorrow, no worries and everything around protects you. We derive our happiness from the people we love. Gradually, all our problems end."

The boys freed the crabs. The villagers and boys gave proper greetings to the Buddha and the Sangha. Buddha left from there with the monks.

2. Adherence to eight virtues (sheela) by ordinary disciples

Once, Buddha was in Shravasti and while addressing the common people, he said,

"Like a layman, monks also have certain responsibilities in their monastic life. Monks live a life of celibacy, so they need to be very careful about their morals. Monks also spend their entire lives in the service and welfare of society."

Here the Buddha is suggesting a way for the lay disciple to experience the bhikkhu's life twice a month. The common disciple can practice the eight precepts once every two weeks.

The common disciple should eat once a day before 12 noon, like the monks and meditate while sitting, walking, and sleeping. On that day, you can invite the bhikkhu to teach the Dhamma. The Buddha said that on that day, one should strictly follow the Panchsheel, which includes abstaining from killing animals, stealing, sexual misconduct, false speech, and intoxication. In addition, there are three other precepts: avoid wearing jewelry, avoid sleeping on a comfortable, high-raised bed, and avoid decorating oneself in order to live a simple life. Similarly, ordinary disciples can also follow Ashtasheel.

The Buddha further stated that happiness and a pleasurable life can be enjoyed in this life only if we follow these guidelines.

The Buddha further said,

- Stay among intelligent people and intellectuals; avoid inferior conduct in life.
- Live in an environment that promotes self-development and moral growth.
- Foster opportunities in which we can work wholeheartedly to practice the Saddhamma and morality.
- Take the time to properly care for your parents, other family members, your spouse and your children.
- Share your success, resources and happiness with others.
- Try to stop the consumption of alcohol and other intoxicants and things that hinder the development of morality.
- Develop a sense of humility, gratitude and try to live a very simple life.
- Create opportunities to get closer to learned monks so that we can develop Saddhamma.
- Try to understand the four noble truths in life and live your life accordingly.

- Spend some time meditating to develop mindfulness and concentration.

3. What is the meaning of Chandal or Fallen and their nature?

Once, when the Buddha was staying in the Jetavana, he went to Shravasti for alms as usual, and stood in front of the house of Bharadvaja Brahmin to seek alms. At that time, a havan ritual was going on at the house of a Bharadvaja Brahmin. Suddenly, his attention was drawn to the Tathagata standing in front of the house. As soon as he saw the Buddha, he shouted angrily.

"O Mundaka, Chandala, Wicked One, why have you come here? "What is your business here?"

Lord Buddha said in a calm and composed voice,

"O Bharadvaja Brahmin, do you know the meaning of Chandala or Fallen and what is called Fallen and do you know what is the nature and religion of a Chandala when he becomes Fallen?"

Bharadvaja, a Brahmin, said to the Buddha,

"I don't know anything about the Fallen and the Chandalas. Please guide me."

Tathagat Buddha said,

"The man who hates others, who is inclined to do evil, who acts arrogantly in life, who accepts imaginary ideas, who does not have kindness, friendship, compassion, love, who always acts with a greedy attitude, one who provokes others unnecessarily, blinded by sinful lust, one who has no fear of committing sin should be considered a Chandala or a Fallen Person."

"The man who gets angry frequently, who takes revenge on others, who earns his living by looting, who is an adulterer, who does not serve his parents, who abuses his own relatives and who lies to hide his sins should be called a Chandala, a Fallen One."

Buddha further said that,

"O Bharadvaja, a person is neither superior nor inferior by birth. A person born into a high caste may become lowly due to their inferior deeds. Being born in a particular caste does not make a person inferior or superior; rather, a person becomes superior or inferior by their words, thoughts, and actions."

Bharadvaja was very satisfied after listening to the teachings of Tathagat Buddha.

Bharadvaja was filled with emotion and said,

"Buddha, the ocean of compassion, friendship and equality, I was wrong. Please excuse me. Tathāgata, I surrender myself to the Buddha, the Dhamma and the Sangha, and from today onwards I will serve these three jewels as long as there is breath in my body. Being your seeker, please forgive my mistake."

4. Best qualities spread in all directions

Once Lord Gautam Buddha was in Jetavana, Shravasti. Buddha asked Ananda to go to Shravasti to complete some important work. Since it was summer, Ananda felt thirsty and wanted to drink some water. He saw a well from which a girl was taking water.

He went to the well and politely asked the girl for water to quench his thirst. However, when she got ready to give water, she remembered her low social status as she belonged to an untouchable, low social caste. She politely said to Ananda,

"Sorry, brother, I cannot give you water because I am polluted, being from the untouchable caste, and I do not want to pollute you."

Bhante Ananda told her,

"He did not ask about her caste, he just wanted water. He believed that every human being is equal."

On his repeated requests, she gave water to Ananda to drink. Ananda was very happy and then started walking.

She was fascinated by Ananda's personality and decided to follow him. Bhante Ananda entered the Buddha's hut, paid obeisance to him, narrated the whole incident, and then went to his own hut.

The girl also entered Buddha's hut, bowed before the Lord, and said.

"Lord, help me. I have fallen deeply in love with Ananda, and I want to stay here. Please allow me to stay here so that I can serve him."

Buddha examined her emotional state and said,

"You are not attracted to him, but you are attracted to his kindness, his kind behavior towards you. I want Ananda's great character to be passed on to you so that you can be kind and compassionate towards others like Ananda."

Buddha further told her that,

"Desire gives rise to attachment and because of attachment we invite suffering. When we destroy craving, it automatically destroys attachment and suffering."

Buddha further explained to her that,

"When a king is kind to his subjects, he is praised everywhere. However, when the subjects are kind to the king, it is more praiseworthy. Similarly, when any charitable and kind deed is done by upper-caste women, it is appreciated. Whereas when the lower caste women do such work, it is appreciated more in the society."

Buddha further said,

"Oh my daughter, you are great. Although you belong to the lower strata of society, you can still attain the highest spiritual, religious and moral status. When you do this, you will become even better than the queen. Your best qualities will spread in all directions like the fragrance of fragrant flowers. You focus on your emotions. You focus more on attaining Nibbana rather than focusing more on pleasure."

After listening to the Buddha, she decided to enter the Bhikkhu order. She told him her wish to the Buddha. However, the Buddha asked her to enter the Bhikkhu order with the permission of her family. After permission from her family members, she very happily joined the Bhikkhu Sangha and became the best Buddha's disciple.

5. What is real wealth in life?

Once, the Buddha was staying in Jetavana. At that time Sri Ugra, the minister of King Prasenajit, came to the Buddha, after due greeting, he took his seat and asked the Buddha.

"I am just returning from a rich man. He has a lot of property. I also want to become very wealthy, but despite being the minister of King Prasenjit, I am very poor."

Buddha replied to Shri Ugra,

"No doubt such wealth is needed by everyone and everyone should have it. However, this type of property always requires protection from thieves, robbers, fire, floods, and many other factors. Therefore, I cannot say that this is the true wealth of a person. The true wealth of a person is faith, morality, social standing, fear of doing wrong, learning, renunciation and knowledge. These are the seven true wealth of any person. The man or woman who has this kind of wealth cannot be called poor."

The Buddha then elaborated on each of these forms of wealth as follows.

- **Faith Wealth**: You must have faith in the teachings of the Buddha, his Dhamma and his Sangha.
- **Moral Wealth**: Not killing, not lying, not committing adultery, not stealing, and avoiding drug abuse are moral principles that

should be adopted by everyone to live a happy and peaceful life.

- **Fear of society**: Always being cautious in doing good deeds and charity, always thinking that doing wrong things will bring dishonor to my family. I have a very good reputation in society and doing bad things will bring disgrace to my family. My social reputation will be harmed.
- **Fear of Doing Wrong**: What will society, people around us and our family think about us if we get involved in wrongdoing? And thinking this, we should avoid bad things in life.
- **Shruti Dhan**: Read and listen to as much factual and informative content as possible that is useful for human welfare. Apply such useful information in the interest of society and in your personal life.
- **Sacrifice**: We should generously donate whatever we can from our possessions without expecting anything in return. Sacrifice not only means giving up money but also giving up one's bad habits, negative thoughts and negative emotions like greed, hatred, anger, and jealousy.
- **Wisdom**: Knowing about the Four Noble Truths, the Eightfold Path, the Ten Paramitas, and the other teachings of the Buddha is the real wealth.

Addressing Minister Sri Ugra, the Buddha said that,

"These seven virtues are real wealth because they cannot be plundered or stolen and do not need any protection. Instead of desiring material wealth, you should desire to bring these virtues into your life, you will be truly rich."

Minister Sri Ugra said,

"Oh my Lord Gautam Buddha, I am truly very grateful to you for giving me advice on real wealth in life. I will continue to serve you throughout my life. I request you to accept me into your Bhikkhu Sangha."

Sri Ugra joined the Bhikku Sangha.

6. Put soil in my alms bowl as alms

Once, the Buddha was residing in Jetavana of Shravasti. After his morning routine, he went to Shravasti for alms. The Buddha used to stand in front of a house every day for alms. A middle-aged woman opened the door and saw the Buddha in front of her. She was very happy, and her happiness had no limits. She saluted the Buddha and suddenly started crying. The Buddha asked the reason for her crying.

She said,

"This is the first time that the Buddha has come to my door for alms and asked me for something in the form of alms, and unfortunately, there is not a single grain of food in my house to offer to the Lord."

She said how unfortunate she was. She was cursing her poverty and poor financial condition.

The Buddha spoke to her in a pitiful voice,

"O mother, please do not beat yourself up for having nothing to give me. I still request you to take some soil from your courtyard and put it in my alms bowl as alms. You should continue your donations, do not stop it at any cost."

She replied,

"Bhante, what you are suggesting is a very unfair thing for me. How can I put soil in your alms bowl and spoil your alms?"

Buddha said,

"It does not matter to me if I go to sleep hungry without eating even for a day. But giving up the habit of donating something to the needy can be a curse for you."

Buddha said,

"O mother, please feel free to put a few handfuls of soil in my bowl, it is not a bad thing. I will gladly accept it. Those who follow the Dhamma never lie, they do not get angry and they donate whatever they can. If we have something to donate, then try to donate some of it. We should not give up the habit of charity."

Although she did not want to do this act, she still put a handful of soil from her courtyard in the Buddha's alms bowl, albeit unwillingly. While committing this act, her heart broke into pieces. But this was the Buddha's order, so she was helpless.

Buddha accepted the donation of a handful of soil and set out for Jetavana.

She was looking towards the Buddha and saying in her mind, "O Lord, please forgive me."

7. Yeshukari Sutta

Once, the Buddha was living in Jetavana. The Yeshukari Brahmin went to the Buddha and exchanged greetings with him. When the greetings and humble conversation ended, he sat on one side and said to the Buddha;

"Guru Siddharth Gautam, Brahmins determine four types of services in society. What are those service?

- One for a Brahmin,
- One for a Noble,
- One for the farmer, and
- One for a person who performs manual labor.

The farmer and the person who does manual labor should serve an elite or king. The one who does manual labor should serve the farmers. Those who do manual labor should serve their own class or caste. However, all these should serve a Brahmin. These are four types of services that Brahmins determine. What do you say about this?"

Buddha smiled and replied,

"But, oh Brahmins, has the whole world authorized Brahmins to determine these four types of services?"

Buddha said,

"All these social rules have been made unilaterally without consulting all stakeholders. Brahmin, I do not say that you should serve everyone, nor do I say that you should not serve anyone. I say that you should not serve anyone if you do not get better but worse by serving them. And I say that you should serve someone if you get better by serving them, not worse."

"If they ask an elite or aristocrat, whom should you serve? There is someone whose service you get worse or someone who gets better in service? Giving the correct answer, an aristocrat would say, there is someone whose service I receive better."

If they ask a Brahmin... farmer... for a person doing physical labor, whom should you serve? There is someone whose service you get worse, or someone who gets better in service? Giving the correct answer, a servant would say, "There is someone whose service I receive better."

"Brahmin, I do not say that you become a better or worse person by coming from a reputed family. I do not say that being very beautiful makes you a better or bad person. I do not say that being very rich makes you a better or bad person. Because some people from prestigious families kill living beings, steal, and commit sexual misconduct. They use speech that is false, divisive, harsh or meaningless. And they are greedy, malicious and wrong-minded. That's why I don't say that coming from a prestigious family or a particular class or caste makes you a more honest person."

"But some people from respectable families also refrain from killing living beings, stealing and sexual misconduct. They avoid using speech that is false, divisive, harsh, or meaningless. Moreover, they are not greedy or malicious and their viewpoint is correct. So I don't say that coming from a prestigious family makes you a worse person."

"People who are very beautiful or not very beautiful, people who are very rich or not very rich, can behave in a similar manner. I'm not saying that any of these things make you a better or worse person."

"Brahmin, I do not say that you should serve everyone, nor do I say that you should not serve anyone. I suggest you should serve someone if serving them increases your faith, morality, education, generosity and knowledge. I say you should not serve anyone if serving them does not increase your faith, morality, education, generosity and knowledge."

When the Buddha completed his address, Yeshukari, the Brahmin, said,

"These are the four types of wealth that Brahmins describe. What do you say about this?"

- The wealth they set aside for the Brahmin is his alms. The Brahmin who despises their wealth is like a guard who steals, that is, they fail in their duty of guarding.
- The wealth they set aside for a noble or a king is the bow and quiver. The noble person who despises their wealth, the bow and quiver, is like a guard who steals, as they fail in their duty of guarding.
- The wealth they determine for a farmer is farming and animal husbandry. The farmer who neglects their farming and animal husbandry is like a guard who steals, as they fail in their duty of guarding.
- The wealth they assign to a person who does manual labor is a sickle and an axe. The person who does manual labor, who despises their sickle and axe, is like a guard who steals, that is, they fail in their duty of guarding.

Buddha said,

"But Brahmins, has the whole world authorized Brahmins to determine these four types of property?"

"No, Lord Gautama, the Brahmins have determined these four types of property without the consent of these four types of people."

Buddha said,

"I declare that a man's own wealth is great and excellent education. Traditionally, we called the particular person a Brahmin, Noble, Farmer, or Manual Labourer belongs from particular social class or caste in which they were born. It is like fire, which is counted according to the condition in which it burns. The fire which burns dependent on logs is considered as log fire. The fire which burns dependent on twigs is considered to be twig fire. The fire which burns dependent on grass is considered grass fire. The fire which burns dependent on cow dung is considered a cow dung fire."

"Suppose someone from a noble or royal family, a farmer or a manual laborer relying on the teachings and training propounded by the enlightened one, abstains from killing living beings, stealing, and sensual pleasures. They avoid using speech that is false, divisive, harsh, or meaningless. And they are not greedy or malicious and their viewpoint is correct. They become successful in their life through an efficient learning system."

"You think only a Brahmin is capable of developing a loving heart free of enmity and malice, and not a noble, a peasant, or a lower class?"

"No, Gautama, persons from Noble or Royal families or Brahmins or Farmers or Manual Workers could all do so. Because all four classes are capable of developing a heart of love free from enmity, malice and hatred."

Next Buddha asked him,

"Brahmin, what do you think? Is only a Brahmin capable of taking a bath, going to the river and washing off the dust and dirt, and not a member of a Noble or Royal family, a Farmer or a Manual Labourer could do so ?"

The Brahmin said,

"No, Guru Gautama. All four classes are capable of doing this."

"Similarly, I declare that a man's own wealth is great and excellent education. However, they are recognized based on the traditional family lineage of their mother and father. In fact, they should be evaluated on the basis of their merit and decent behavior in society."

After this discussion, Yeshukari Brahmin said to the Buddha,

"Very well, Gautama! Excellent! From today onwards, Guru Gautama, remember me as an ordinary follower who has come under your protection throughout my life. "

8. No one is superior by birth

When the Buddha was once residing in Jetavana, a man named Avadhgupta, a self-proclaimed intellectual came to the Buddha to debate some issues. After proper salutation, he sat on one side and prepared himself to say something to the Buddha.

He said,

"O Gautama, I have come here to learn from you about the benefits of the Chaturvarna system, which is very beautifully designed, which is very useful for the society because it is based on division of labour. Please give your opinion on it."

Buddha replied to this self-proclaimed intellectual, saying,

"The Chaturvarna system in the society is the result of a crooked and bad mentality. This system is completely responsible for division in the society, hence the society is fragmented. If the social system is so good, then it should be followed in every country and region of the world. If we talk about other surrounding states, there are only two social classes: slaves and masters. But they are also transferable. Today's slave can become a tomorrow's master."

Avadhgupta said,

"Have you heard that any Shudra in the society has attained Brahmatva in his life or any ignorant Brahmin has served any Shudra person."

Buddha said, "O Avadhgupta, when all women give birth to a child, the name of any caste is not applied to that child; rather, it is a human being. Then how does one person become inferior by birth and another superior? All persons are equal by birth. They achieve greatness on the basis of their good deeds in life. No one is a Shudra, an Untouchable, or a Brahmin by birth; only personal actions are responsible for one's status in the society."

Buddha further said,

"My dear friend, every person needs to adopt the following actions in their life for self-welfare.

- Faith.

- Health.
- Honesty.
- Energy.
- Knowledge.

Any person of any caste can get it. There should be no inherent difference in the attainment of these five qualities. Just as trained elephants and horses perform better in war than untrained ones, those who are properly trained can perform better and live a happier life. Anyone who is properly trained can perform better and live a happier life."

"O wise man, the Chaturvarna system in society is unnatural, harmful, and undesirable. If people of all four castes bring dry branches and burn them, can you say the flames coming out of them will be of different colors? Will you say this flame is of a Shudra, Brahmin, rich, or poor, inferior, or superior person? Wouldn't each of them provide the same light, same heat, and same flame?"

"If there is a lack of liberty, fraternity, equality and justice in society, how can we say that it is a progressive, ideal and visionary society? A person who lacks love, friendship, compassion and equanimity cannot be called an intelligent person. Similarly, a religion which preaches caste, ignorance, untruth, false rituals and divisions between humans cannot be considered an ideal and progressive religion."

"It is not important to be born in a so-called higher caste or varna, but it is better to have high ideals. Inequality, hatred and a feeling of superiority do not help progress in any country or society. All human beings are equal without any discrimination. Therefore, an intelligent person should strive to establish an ideal society."

Hearing the Buddha's words, all the people present with Avadhgupta were pleased and requested the Buddha to include them in his Sangha. Everyone was admitted into the Sangha.

9. Legitimate causes of human downfall

Once, Buddha was residing in Jetavana. Some people came to him and requested that the Buddha to tell them something about the causes of human downfall.

After proper greetings, the Buddha said:

- People who love their enemies more than their loved ones. When people are more interested in the welfare of their enemies than that of their own family members and relatives, the downfall of such a person is certain.
- People who are lazy, sleepy or idle and live with bad, foolish, and angry people often lack energy, their downfall is certain.
- Those who do not donate to monks or the needy, despite having the ability to donate or avoid donating by lying, the downfall of such person is certain.
- A person who enjoys all the luxuries, wealth and worldly pleasures, high-quality food alone, and does not share with their loved ones, the downfall of such a person is certain.
- The person who is overly proud of their wealth, achievements, caste, or religion, the downfall of such people is certain.
- People who hate and insult their community members, relatives and brothers, the downfall of such people is certain.
- A person who commits adultery, is not satisfied with their married partner, always indulges in prostitution, consumes all kinds of intoxicants, plays cards and wastes their wealth, the downfall of such a person is certain.
- An elderly man who is married to a young girl is unable to sleep peacefully. This is the reason for their sorrow and lamentation; the downfall of such a person is certain.
- The person during their lifetime transfers their property to an undisciplined son or a misbehaving wife, their downfall is certain.
- Those who are poor and unable to support their families are often very proud of their caste, gotra, and community. Due to this false

ego, they are unable to engage in meaningful work and earn enough to support themselves. This is the reason for their sorrow. The downfall of such a person is certain.

Buddha concluded his sermon by saying,

"Those who understand my Dhamma teachings are not humiliated in their lives. Those who follow the Dhamma teachings are always ahead of those who do not follow it. The wise person identifies the causes of human downfall and tries to avoid them. Therefore, each of us must follow the noble path of life."

10. Four types of people

In Shravasti, on one occasion, the Buddha beautifully explained the difference between right and wrong conduct of the people to ordinary disciples in a discourse. Buddha addressed his disciples and said there are four kinds of people.

- The first kind of person is the most foolish kind of person, one who has acquired wealth through deceit and fraud and does not use it to support themselves or for others.
- The second type of person earns money through deceit and uses that money at least for themselves and their relatives.
- The third type of person is more intelligent and uses the money earned through deceit for the happiness of others.
- The fourth type of person is one who condemns those who earn money through deceit and illegal means. A fully aware person observes every human behavior minutely.

Buddha further said there are two types of people:

- People who are strongly attached and fascinated by their wealth, unaware of its inherent danger, do not find a way to come out of it. Such individuals do not experience peace and contentment in their lives.
- There are some who are not attached to their wealth, are not fascinated by it, are aware of its inherent dangers, and know their way out. This second type of people enjoys worldly pleasures and happiness derived from money.

11. With Accountant Moggalana

Once when the Buddha was staying at the Pubbarama monastery built by Vishakha in Shravasti, Moggallana, a Brahmin Accountant by profession, approached the Buddha and exchanged greetings with him. When the greetings and polite conversation were over, he sat aside and said to the Buddha.

"Lord Gautama, in this monastery we can see a gradual progression of stairs from bottom to top. Among the Brahmins, we can see gradual progress in learning the Vedas. Among archers, we can see gradual progress in archery. Among us accountants, who make a living by accounting, we can see gradual progress in mathematics. Is it possible to describe gradual training, gradual progress and gradual practice in your teaching and training for monks?"

Buddha explained to him that it is possible, Brahmin. When an Enlightened One finds someone to train, they first guide them thus: come monk, be moral and disciplined in the monastic code, keep your conduct good, and beg for alms at suitable places. Seeing the danger in even the slightest mistake, follow the rules you have adopted.

When they practice ethical conduct, an Enlightened One guides them further: come monk, guard your sense doors. When you see a scene with your own eyes, don't get caught up in its features and details. If the ability to see is left uncontrolled, bad unskillful qualities like greed and unhappiness will take over. For this reason, practice restraint, protect the ability to see and gain control over it. When you hear a sound with your ears, when you smell with your nose, when you taste a flavor with your tongue, when you feel touch with your body, don't get trapped in characteristics. If the mind is left unbridled, the bad unskillful qualities of greed and unhappiness will become overwhelming. For this reason, practice restraint, protect the capacity of the mind, and achieve its control.

When they guard their sense doors, an Enlightened One directs them further: come monk, eat with moderation. Consider the food you eat rationally: eat not for pleasure, indulgence or adornment, but only to maintain this body, avoid harm and support spiritual practice.

When they eat with moderation, an Enlightened One guides them further: come monk, commit yourself to awakening. Practice meditation while walking and sitting to clear your mind of obstructions. Continue your walking and sitting meditation practice in the evening. At midnight, lie down on your right side in lion posture, placing one leg over the other and meditate. Get up in the early hours of the night and continue practicing meditation while walking to clear your mind of distractions.

When they are committed to awakening, an Enlightened One guides them further: come monk, have mindfulness and situational awareness. Exercise situational awareness when going out and coming back. When looking forward and to the side, observe awareness while bending and extending the limbs, while wearing outer wear, both shoes, while eating, drinking, chewing and tasting, while urinating and defecating, while walking, standing, sitting, sleeping, waking up, speaking and remaining silent.

When they have mindfulness and situational awareness, an Enlightened One directs them further: come monk, concentrate the mind in a solitary dwelling, in a forest, under a tree, on a hill, in a mountain cave, in the open air or in a secluded place.

When they return from alms giving, an Enlightened One asks them to sit cross-legged after meals, keep their body straight, and establish meditation. By giving up the greed of the world, they meditate with a heart free from greed, purifying the mind from greed. By giving up ill will and malice, they meditate with a mind filled with compassion for all living beings. They meditate with a mind free from lethargy and drowsiness, they meditate without any restlessness, their mind is peaceful from within. By giving up doubt, they meditate by going beyond doubt and freeing the mind from doubt.

They give up these five hindrances that weaken the intellect and the evil thoughts that come to mind. Then, they give up sensual pleasures and unskillful qualities. They enter and remain in the first stage of meditation, in which they concentrate and engage the mind, enjoying the euphoria and joy generated by solitude. They enter and remain in the second stage of meditation, where there is joy with the extinction of rapture. They enter and remain in the third stage of meditation, where they meditate with equanimity and mental tranquility. By renouncing pleasures and pains and by ending suffering, they enter and remain in the fourth stage of meditation."s

The accountant Moggallana said to the Buddha,

"When disciples are instructed and advised by Lord Gautama in this way, do they all achieve the ultimate goal or do some of them fail?"

Buddha said, "Some succeed, while others fail."

Accountant Moggalana said,

"Among all types of aromatic roots, Jatamansi is considered the best; of all the types of aromatic sandalwood, red sandalwood is considered the best; Jasmine is considered the best among all types of fragrant flowers. Similarly, the advice of Lord Gautama is the best in contemporary teachings."

Well done, Lord Gautama! Excellent!

"You are righting the inverted, uncovering the hidden, pointing the way to the lost, lighting a lamp in the darkness so that those with clear eyes may see what is there."

"You have clarified the teachings in many ways. I take refuge in Lord Gautama, his Dhamma and his order of Bhikkhu Sangha. From today onwards, may Lord Gautama accept me as a follower who has taken refuge in Him for life."

12. Pothapada Sutta: States of Consciousness

Once the Buddha was staying in Jetavana Park in Shravasti. At that time, the traveler Pothapada, along with about three hundred travellers was staying in the Shastrartha room in the garden of Queen Mallika.

Buddha got up early, wore his robes, took the bowl with him, and decided to go to Shravasti to beg for alms. But he remembered that it was too early to go to Shravasti and he decided to go to the debate room to meet the traveler Pothapada.

There, Pothapada was sitting with his crowd of wanderers, all shouting and making a lot of noise, carrying on all kinds of indecent conversations in vulgar language.

They were all discussing kings, robbers, ministers, armies, dangers, wars, food, drinks, clothes, beds, garlands, perfumes, relatives, villages, towns, cities, countries, women, heroes, roads, and much more. Gossip and insulting conversations, speculations about land and sea, and talk of being and not being.

Pothapada saw the Lord Buddha coming from a distance, so he called his followers.

"Be quiet, gentlemen, do not make any noise. The ascetic Gautama is coming, and he likes peace and speaks in praise of it. If he sees that these people are peaceful, he will probably want to come and meet us."

The people became silent in response.

Pothapada welcomed the Buddha, "Come, Venerable Lord, welcome, Venerable Lord, sit down Lord, the seat is ready."

Buddha sat on the prepared seat, and Pothapada took a low seat and sat on one side.

Buddha said,

"Pothapada, what were you all talking about? Have I interrupted your conversation?"

Pothapada replied,

"In the last few days, ascetics and Brahmins of different sects have sat together and discussed the extinction of higher consciousness and how it comes about."

"Some people said, person's perceptions arise and cease without any cause or condition. When it arises, the person is conscious; when it ceases, the person is unconscious."

This is how he explained it, but someone else said,

"No, it is not so. Perceptions are a person's own nature, which keep coming and going. When it comes, it is conscious; when it goes, it is unconscious. Said another.

That is not accurate; there are ascetics and Brahmins with great powers who conclude that consciousness resides within man and can be drawn out. When they draw him in, he is conscious; when they draw him out, he is unconscious.

And the other one said that is not the case. There is no god or supernatural power with great powers; they merely insert and remove consciousness in man with great effect. When they put him in it, he is conscious; when they take him out, he is unconscious."

"I thought about you in this connection. I am sure only you can explain these different concepts correctly." Pothapada said.

Buddha said,

"Ah, Pothapada, certainly, in this case those ascetics and Brahmins who say that one's perceptions arise and cease without any cause or condition are completely wrong. Why is it so? A person's perceptions arise and are eliminated due to specific causes and conditions. Some perceptions arise through meditation training and some are eliminated through meditation training."

Pothapada asked, "What is this training?"

"The ascetics or monks who are adept in virtuous conduct see no danger from any side. In this manner, they become proficient in good conduct. He guards his senses. This indicates that they have full control over their senses.

After attaining the first stage of meditation, they remain established in it. And any previous feelings of lust they had also disappeared. At that time, a genuine yet subtle feeling of joy and happiness arising from renunciation is present, and the person is aware of this happiness. Thus, some beliefs arise through training, and other beliefs are eliminated through training. And this is the training of meditation.

Then, the Bhikkhu, having attained inner peace and mental concentration, with a tranquil mind and thoughts, reaches and remains in the second stage of meditation, which is free from thinking and thought, filled with concentration and happiness. His previous genuine yet subtle perception of the joy and happiness arising from renunciation disappears. In this meditative state, there is a genuine yet subtle feeling of happiness arising from concentration. The person becomes conscious of this happiness. Thus, some beliefs arise through meditation training, and some are eliminated through meditation training.

Then, after the pleasant sensation disappears, the practitioner remains in equanimity, conscious and clearly aware and they experience pleasant, unpleasant, and neutral bodily sensations. The person remains happy; they reach the third state of meditation and remain there. In this state, a genuine yet subtle feeling of equanimity and happiness arises. He lives in this genuine yet subtle feeling of equanimity and happiness. Thus, some beliefs arise through meditation training, and some are eliminated through meditation training.

Then, with the abandonment of pleasure and pain, and the disappearance of previous pleasure and pain, they reach and remain in the fourth stage of meditation, a state beyond pleasure and pain, purified by equanimity and mindfulness.

His previous genuine yet subtle feeling of equanimity and happiness disappears, and a genuine yet subtle feeling of neither happiness nor sadness arises, and they become a person who feels neither happiness nor sadness. He is aware of these true but subtle emotions. Thus, some notions arise through meditation training, and some are eliminated through meditation training.

Then, by going completely beyond physical sensations and by the disappearance of all feelings of resistance and non-aversion to the perception of diversity, they reach and live in the region of infinite space. Thus, some beliefs arise through meditation training, and some are eliminated through meditation training.

Then, going completely beyond the region of infinite space, seeing that consciousness is infinite, they reach and remain in the region of infinite consciousness. Thus, some beliefs arise through meditation training, and some are eliminated through meditation training.

Again, going completely beyond the region of infinite consciousness, seeing that there is nothing, they reach and remain in the region of nothingness, and they become what it truly is. Remains conscious of these subtle senses. Thus, some beliefs arise through meditation training, and some are eliminated through meditation training.

Pothapada, from the moment the monk has attained this controlled perception, he progresses from one stage to another until he reaches the limit of perception.

When they reach the limit of perception, the following occurs to them:

Mental activities are worse for me; a lack of mental activities is better. He thinks and imagines that the notions he has acquired will come to an end, and coarse thoughts will arise within him.

Therefore, he neither thinks nor imagines. Then, only these concepts arise in him; other gross concepts do not arise and he attains the state of equanimity.

And Pothapada, it is the way in which the cessation of perception occurs by successive stages."

"What do you think, Pothapada? Have you heard about it before?"

"No Gautama, as I understand it,"

Buddha said again:

"Therefore, he neither thinks nor imagines. But other, coarser thoughts do not arise. He attains the complete state of cessation of disturbance and distress in the mind. This is the method in which perception is accomplished by successive stages."

"What do you think, Pothapada? Have you heard about it before?"

"No, Gautama, as I understand it."

Buddha further said,

"Pothapada, from the moment a Bhikkhu has attained this controlled perception, he progresses from one stage to another, and when he reaches the limit of perception, he attains cessation. In this way, the notion of successive stages ends."

"Is that right, Pothapada."

"Lord, do you teach whether experience is one or many?"

"I teach it as both one and many."

"O Lord, how is this one and how are there many?"

"Just as he successively attains the cessation of each perception, so I teach the peak of that perception: thus I teach one peak of perception, and I also teach many."

"Lord, does understanding arise before knowledge or does knowledge arise before understanding or do both arise together?"

"First, understanding arises, Pothapada, then knowledge, and from the arising of understanding comes knowledge."

"Lord, is the perception of 'self' of the person, or is the perception one thing, and the 'self' is something else?"

"Well, Pothapada, do you imagine yourself?"

"Lord, my 'self' is gross, material, made up of the five elements (earth, fire, water, air and space) and dependent on solid food."

"But with such a gross 'self', Pothapada, perception would be one thing, and 'self' would be another thing."

"You can look at it like this. Looking at such a gross 'self', certain notions will arise in a person, and others will cease. Thus, you can see that the perception must be one thing, the 'self' is another."

"O Lord, I consider the mind-created concept of 'self' to be perfect in all its parts, with no defect in any of the sense organs."

Pothapada said, "But with such a mind-created 'self', perception would be one thing, and the 'self' another. Buddha, O my Lord, I believe in a formless soul, made up of perception."

The Buddha said, "But with such a formless 'self', perception would be one thing, and the 'self' something else."

Pothapada said, "But Lord, is it possible for me to know whether perception is a person's 'self' or whether perception is one thing, and 'self' another thing?"

Buddha said,

"Pothapada, it is difficult for a person with different views, different beliefs, different influences, different goals, and different training to know if these are two different things."

Pothapada said, "Okay, Lord, if this question of 'self' and perceptions is difficult for a person like me - then tell me: is the world eternal? Is this the only truth or a lie?"

The Buddha said, "Pothapada, I have not declared that the world is eternal, and the contrary view is wrong."

"Well Gautama, isn't the world eternal?"

Buddha said, "I have not declared that the world is not eternal."

"Okay Gautama, is the world infinite or is it not infinite?"

"I have not declared that the world is not infinite and that the opposite view is wrong."

"Well Lord, are the soul and the body the same,... is the soul one thing and the body another?"

"I have not declared that the soul is one thing and the body is another."

"Well, Lord, do the Tathāgatas continue to live even after death? Is this the only truth and everything else is a lie?"

"I have not declared that the Tathagata continues to live even after death."

"Okay Lord, does Tathagata exist after death or not?"

"I have not declared whether the Tathagata exists after death or not."

"But why did the Lord not declare these things?"

"Pothapada, this thing is not fit for purpose, not conducive to the Dhamma and not the way to begin a holy life. By not declaring whether the Tathagata will continue to exist after death does not lead to disillusionment, renunciation, cessation or hinder peace, higher knowledge, enlightenment and nibbana."

"That's why I have not announced it."

"But O Lord, what has the Lord announced?"

"Pothapada, Yes, I have declared many things."

"I declare that in life there is suffering, there is the origin of suffering, there is the end of suffering, and there are paths leading to the end of suffering."

"But, Lord, why has the Lord declared this?"

"Because, Pothapada, it is conducive to the purpose, conducive to the Dhamma, the way to begin the sacred life; it leads to disillusionment, to renunciation, to cessation, to peace, to higher knowledge, to enlightenment, to nibbana. That is why I have made this announcement."

Pothapada was extremely satisfied with the answer he received from the Buddha and said,

"O Lord, we thank you very much for such a good explanation on various issues and now we would like to take leave from you."

Then, the Buddha got up from his place and left after giving proper greetings.

Then, as soon as the Lord had left, pilgrims from all sides turned to Pothapada, mocked him and spoke derisively.

"Pothapada, do you agree with whatever the ascetic Gautam says? We could not understand a single word of the entire sermon of the ascetic Gautam. Is the world eternal or not? Is it finite or infinite? Is the soul the same as or different from the body? - Is there existence after death or not?"

Pothapada replied:

"I don't even understand whether the world is eternal or not, or whether the Tathagata exists after death or not. But the ascetic Gautama teaches a true and genuine way of practice that is in accordance with the

Dhamma. And why should someone like me not approve of the true and genuine practice so well taught by the ascetic Gautama?"

12. Building of stairs for a palace at the crossroads

Two or three days later, the elephant-trainer's son named Chitta went with Pothapada to see the Lord Buddha. Chitta bowed before the Buddha and sat down.

Pothapada exchanged courtesies with the Lord Gautama and sat aside, and told him what had happened.

The Buddha said,

"Pothapada, all those travelers are blind and sightless. Among them, you are also sightless. Pothapada, I have taught and explained some things, some as being certain, some as being uncertain. What are those things that I mentioned as uncertain? The world is declared to be indeterminate... whether the Tathagata exists even after death or not..."

"Why? Because they are not conducive to Nibbana. That is why I have declared them uncertain."

"But what things have I said with certainty?"

"There is suffering, there is the origin of suffering, there is the cessation of suffering, and there is the path to the cessation of suffering."

"Why? Because they are suited to the purpose, suited to the Dhamma, suited to the path of beginning a holy life. They lead to disillusionment, renunciation, cessation of suffering, peace, higher knowledge, enlightenment, and nibbana. That is why I have declared them certain."

The Buddha further said,

"Pothapada, there are some ascetics and Brahmins who declare and believe that after death the soul becomes completely happy and free from disease.

I contacted them and asked if this was really what he declared and believed, and he replied: "Yes."

Then I said, "Friends, while living in this world, know and see it as a completely happy place?" And they answered: "No."

I said, "Have you ever experienced a night or day, or midnight or day, that was completely happy?" And they replied: "No."

I said, "Do you know or practice any way that could bring about a completely happier world?" And they replied: "No."

I said, "Have you heard the voice of the gods who have been reborn in a completely happy world, saying: I have been born in a completely happy world and, gentlemen, have been reborn in a happy realm?" And they replied, "No."

The Buddha continued, "What do you think, Pothapada? In such a situation, don't the words of those sages and Brahmins become foolish?"

'It's like a man saying that, "I'm going to find the most beautiful girl in the country and make love to her."

They can tell him.

"Well, do you know about this most beautiful girl of the country, which class, caste she belongs to, where she lives, what she does, who are her parents? Is she from the Kshatriya, Brahmin, merchant, or artisan class?" And he will say: "No, I do not know about that in detail."

Then they can say.

"Well, do you know her name, her gotra? Whether she is tall or short or of medium height? whether she is dark or fair-skinned? She is which village, town or city does she come from? Whether, she has high, low or medium height?"

And he will say: "No."

"Does the man's words sound unbelievable?"

"Certainly, Buddha"

"And so it is with the sages and Brahmins who declare and believe that after death the soul is completely free from pleasure and disease. Do their words not prove to be foolishness?"

"Certainly, Lord."

"It's like a man building stairs for a palace at the crossroads."

People may say to him, "Okay, now, for the palace for which you are making this staircase - do you know whether the palace will be on the east side, the west side, the north side or the south side?"

"Certainly, Lord."

And at these words, the traveler Pothapada said to the Lord.

"Excellent, Lord, excellent. It is like someone lifting up a discouraged person or showing the way to someone who is lost or bringing an oil lamp into a dark place, so that those with eyes can see what is there."

Similarly, Gautam Buddha has explained Dhamma in different ways.

Pothapada said,

"O Lord, I take refuge in the Buddha, the Dhamma, and the Sangha. "May the Lord accept me as a follower who has taken refuge in the Buddha, the Dhamma, and the Sangha from today until the end of my life!"

Similarly, Citta said to Buddha,

"Lord, I take refuge in the Buddha, the Dhamma, and the Sangha. O Lord, may I attain the path of advancement at the hands of the Buddha, may I attain initiation."

And Chitta, the son of the elephant-trainer, entered the Dhamma stream from the hands of the Lord Buddha, and he became one of the Arhats.

13. Other Suttas delivered by the Buddha in Shravasti

- There is nothing that brings as much harm and suffering as an undeveloped and uncultured mind. A developed and cultured mind brings happiness and many benefits.
- Nothing changes as fast as the brain. The mind is intrinsically pure and bright if it is not contaminated by greed, hatred and ignorance.

- If a monk meditates on loving-kindness, developing it even for a short period, he is considered to be following the Buddha's teaching and acting in accordance with his instructions.
- For people who are in the Sotapanna state, it is important to have the right thinking that nothing in nature is permanent.
- If conscious thinking is developed, it can calm the body, the mind becomes calm, rational thinking develops, ignorance goes away, knowledge arises, the illusion of 'self' ends, bad tendencies disappear and bondage is released.
- Two things have to be kept in mind: not being satisfied with what has been achieved in the process of development and resolving to struggle continuously and steadfastly until the goal of enlightenment is achieved.
- Man has two abilities: to do good and to do bad. Renunciation of evil is possible. Renouncing evil brings immense benefits and happiness. Development of good things is also possible. Development of goodness itself brings benefits like a healthy mind and happiness.
- Two things are helpful in attaining liberation in two ways: concentration meditation and insight meditation. If concentration develops, the mind develops and passions go away, resulting in the liberation of the unhealthy mind. If insight develops, wisdom develops, and ignorance goes away.
- There are two people whose debt can never be repaid. One is the mother, and the other is the father. Even if one lives for a hundred years and during this time serves their parents daily, focusing all their attention, love, and personal service on them, someone will still be required to nurture and guide them in this life. The debt can never be repaid.
- However, the immense debt owed to one's mother and father can be repaid. How? If a person convinces their non-believing parents to become Dhamma followers and join the Buddha, the Dhamma, and the Sangha. If they instill morality in their parents, who do not follow it. If they make their miserly parents generous so they share

their wealth with the poor and needy. If he educates his ignorant parents in the knowledge of the four noble truths.

- There are many types of happiness, including the happiness of family life and the happiness of renunciation. The happiness of renunciation is considered the highest. The happiness of sacrifice and mental happiness are also considered the best.
- A foolish person can be recognized by three things: their actions, words, and behavior. Similarly, an intelligent person can be recognized by three things: their deeds, words, and conduct.
- A person is considered poor and destitute if they do not believe in meritorious things, have no shame or self-control, and lack understanding of what is good or bad.
- Other than women, there is no sight, sound, smell, taste or touch that can so captivate and distract a person's mind. In contrast, there is no sight, sound, smell, taste or touch other than that of man that can fascinate and distract women's minds.
- Wherever the karma done out of greed, hatred and ignorance ripens, the person will go there, and the karma ripens, the person will receive the result (vipaka) of that karma.

❖ **Three types of people in the world**

- One type is a person with a mind like an open wound, who is very irritable and displays anger, hatred and irritability.
- Another type is a person with a mind like a flash of lightning, who has correctly understood the Four Noble Truths.
- The third type is a person with a mind like a diamond, who has destroyed the impurities of the mind and realized the liberation of the mind through knowledge.

❖ **Words we speak**

- One type speaks foul-smelling words.
- Another type speaks fragrant words.
- The third type speaks sweet words like honey.

- ❖ **Fundamental causes for the origin of karma**
  - Greed.
  - Hatred.
  - Ignorance.
- ❖ **Not to prevents from giving donation**
  - He impedes the charitable work of the donor.
  - He prevents the recipient from receiving the gift.
  - He weakens and undermines his own generosity and character.
- ❖ **The three dangers**
  - Old age.
  - Sickness.
  - Death.
- ❖ **To deal with any kind of question**
  - Some questions should be answered directly.
  - Others should be answered by analyzing them.
  - Some questions should be answered by counter questions.
  - Finally, some questions should simply be set aside or ignored.
- ❖ **There are four things that no one can change**
  - What is decaying should not decay.
  - What cannot fall ill, can become ill.
  - What is worth living should not die.
  - Any bad deeds should not yield consequences.
- ❖ **Evaluate people in four ways**
  - A thoughtful and intelligent person can be judged by observing them closely after living with them for a quite long time.
  - A thoughtful and intelligent person can judge anyone's integrity by dealing with them and paying close attention over a long period of time.

- Their steadfastness can be judged by a thoughtful and intelligent person by observing them closely in times of adversity.
- A person's intelligence can be assessed by a thoughtful and perceptive person through extended conversations on various subjects.

❖ **Factors that foster the development of wisdom**
- Associating with good people.
- Listening to good Dhamma.
- Maintaining the right view of the mind.
- Living life according to the Buddha's teachings.
- One must possess strengths.
- Higher wisdom.
- Confidence,
- Shame in doing evil.
- Feeling shame in doing bad things.
- Moral conscience.
- Energy.
- Training for insight and wisdom.

❖ **Four contemplations that should be practiced by everyone**
- I am certain to grow old; I cannot avoid aging.
- I am certain to have diseases; I cannot avoid illness.
- I am certain to die; I cannot avoid my death.
- All beloved things do not last. They are subject to change and separation.

Whatever karma I do, good or bad, I shall inherit them. My good karma is my real wealth, and the karma of the past and present is a part of it. Karma is my only inheritance, karma is the only reason for my existence, karma is my kin, my only security.

- ❖ **Standards while preaching and teaching the Dhamma**
  - The Dhamma should be taught through a series of successive discourses.
  - Dhamma should be presented in the form of a rational discourse.
  - Dhamma should be given with compassion and empathy.
  - Dhamma should not be given for worldly gain or advantage.
  - Dhamma should be taught without any reference to self or others.

- ❖ **Removal of grievances or resentments**
  - If resentment arises against a person, one should develop loving-kindness, compassion or equanimity towards them.
  - One should not pay any attention to it or give it any thought.

- ❖ **Things that are extremely important in life**
  - See the Tathagata or the disciples of the Tathagata.
  - The best things we should hear are the Dhamma from the Tathagata or his disciples.
  - The greatest benefit is expressing faith in the Tathagata or their disciples.
  - The best teaching is to impart the highest virtues, cultivate the highest mind and develop the highest wisdom.
  - The best service is to serve the Tathagata or their disciples.
  - The best contemplation: Contemplating the virtues of the Tathagata or their disciples.

- ❖ **Things that can bring suffering to our personal lives**
  - Indulging in sensual pleasures is unwise.
  - Poverty.
  - Indebtedness.
  - The burden of unpaid interest.

- Being demanded to repay creditors.
- Being pressured and harassed by lenders is a burden to be avoided.
- Imprisonment.

❖ **Steps to liberation from suffering**
- A control on senses provides the foundation for morality.
- Morality establishes the groundwork for right conduct.
- Right concentration enables the understanding of the true nature of physical and mental phenomena.
- Understanding the true nature of physical and mental phenomena leads to the cessation of delusion and attachment.
- With the cessation of delusion and attachment, the knowledge and vision of liberation emerge.

❖ **Rare occurrences in the world**
- The appearance in the world of a fully enlightened Buddha is rare.
- Being born among the nobility is rare.
- Having unimpaired physical and mental faculties is rare.
- To be free from stupidity and ignorance is uncommon.
- It is uncommon to be endowed with the desire to perform good deeds.
- A person who expresses gratitude to those who have assisted them is uncommon in the world.

❖ **Different powers**
- The power of a child lies in their ability to cry.
- The power of a woman lies in her anger.
- The power of a robber lies in their strength.
- The power of a king lies in their sovereignty.
- The power of a fool lies in their tongue.

- The power of a wise person is in carefully considering the pros and cons.
- The power of a wise person lies in their wisdom.
- The power of a monk lies in their patience and tolerance.

❖ **Speech that the Buddha has called right speech**
- If they have not seen, they say, I have not seen.
- If they have not heard, they say, I have not heard.
- When they do not realize, they say that, they have not realized.
- Even when they do not know, they say, I do not know.
- When they see, they say, I have seen.
- When they have heard, they say, I have heard.
- When he realizes, he says that he has realized.
- After knowing, they say, I have known.

❖ **Causes that can lead to hatred**
- They have harmed me.
- They are harming me.
- They may harm me.
- They have harmed one of my loved ones.
- They are harming one of my loved ones.
- They may harm one of my loved ones.
- They have done well for a person I dislike.
- They are doing well for a person I dislike.
- They will do well for a person I dislike.

❖ **Qualities must be eliminated**
- Lust.
- Ill will or hatred.
- Ignorance.
- Anger.

- Jealousy.
- Ingratitude.
- Hatred.
- Depraved mentality.

❖ **Living in morality**
- One who follows morality is happy.
- One who is happy feels joy.
- When one feels happy, they are satisfied.
- Being happily satisfied, they become calm and feel content.
- When one feels happy, their mind becomes concentrated.
- With a concentrated mind, they see things as they truly are.
- Seeing things as they truly are develops indifference and detachment towards them.
- Where there is no passion or attachment, with this one attains liberation of the mind from all bondage and enjoys eternal happiness.

❖ **Righteous efforts**
- Energetic efforts to develop and bring to perfection good, healthy states of mind that have already arisen. This involves trying to prevent unhealthy mental states from arising that have not yet arisen. Practitioners focus on protecting their minds from negative thoughts, feelings, and actions such as greed, hatred, delusion, mindfulness, ethical conduct and other skillful means.
- Effort to renounce: Energetic efforts to eliminate unhealthy mental states that have already arisen. This effort focuses on abandoning unhealthy mental states that have already arisen. One works on identifying, acknowledging and letting go of any negative thoughts, feelings or behaviors that are present in one's mind. This process often involves meditation and other practices aimed at cultivating insight and self-awareness.

- Effort to develop: Energetic efforts to cultivate positive, healthy mental states that have not yet arisen. This involves trying to develop wholesome mental states that have not yet arisen. One works on developing positive qualities such as generosity, loving-kindness, compassion, and wisdom through various practices, including meditation, contemplation and acts of service.
- Maintenance effort: Energetic effort to prevent harmful, unhealthy mental states from arising. This effort focuses on maintaining and enhancing the healthy mental states that have already been developed. Practitioners strive to nurture and strengthen their positive qualities, ensuring they remain stable and continue to grow. This includes regular meditation, mindfulness and continued engagement in wholesome activities.

II. Address to King Prasenjit

1. Things that should not be looked down

The first time when King Prasenjit met the Buddha, he asked,

"How is it that Gautama claims to have attained perfect enlightenment? Gautama is as young as a monk."

The Buddha replied,

"Great King, there are five things that should not be looked down upon and despised:

- Youth
- Warriors
- Serpents
- Fire, and
- Bhikkhu (monk)

An angry young warrior can ruthlessly harm others. Even the bite of a small snake can cause death. A small fire can become a huge disaster that destroys buildings and forests. A young hermit can also become a saint."

2. Victory breeds hatred

When Kosala King Prasenjit lost a battle to King Ajatashatru of Magadha and had to return to his capital Shravasti, he went to the Buddha in a dejected state. The Buddha told King Prasenjit that,

"Neither the victor nor the vanquished experience peace. Victory breeds hatred. The vanquished lives in pain."

Later the two kings fought again and Kosal King Prasenjit not only won but also captured his nephew King Ajatashatru alive along with all his elephants, chariots, horses and soldiers. Kosala King Prasenjit thought that he would spare the young king but not his horses, elephants, and others. He wanted to earn the satisfaction out of keeping these material possessions as a prize of victory.

Hearing about this, the Buddha told his disciples that it would be wise for Kosal King Prasenjit to keep nothing for himself. The truth of this statement still applies today in this modern war-weary world.

3. Food should be nutritious

One day, King Prasenjit went to Jetavana to meet the Buddha.

The Buddha requested the King to come to his hut. Coming to the hut, King Prasenjit said,

"Tathagat Buddha, I am now seventy years old. I want to spend more time in spiritual practice. I will practice more than before, but state affairs demand more labor and time. Sometimes when I come to listen to Dhamma discourses, I am so tired that I cannot keep my eyes open, I always feel sleepy."

Buddha smiled,

"Yes, I know. For this, you should eat food in small quantities, but it should be nutritious too. This will keep your mind and body light. You should ask Queen Mallika or the Princess to take care of your meals."

The King said with folded hands.

"I listen to you carefully, my death is near. Keeping this in mind, I think it will be beneficial for me to spend the rest of my life according to your teachings."

King Prasenjit got up, bowed to the Buddha three times, and left feeling satisfied.

4. Loving your subjects like your sons or daughters

Once, Tathagata Gautama Buddha was residing in Jetavan. King Prasenjit came to meet the Buddha. After offering proper greetings and obeisances, he sat down near the Buddha.

He said,

"Tathagat, our kingdom has become sacred by your being with us. Lord, I am blessed by your sight, now I want to hear something on Dhamma."

The Buddha recognized the emotional state of the king. The king appeared quite disappointed.

The Buddha said,

"O King, the wealth, prestige and material things that you have are quite dynamic in nature, which means they are changing with time. However, the wealth of the Dhamma is permanent. A king living in opulence can be much more unhappy than an ordinary person. O King, our bad or wrong deeds follow us like our shadows. A compassionate heart is needed today. As a king, you must love your subjects like your own sons or daughters, protect them and not exploit them. We need to control our thoughts and our senses. Give up evil thinking and adopt good thinking. Give good treatment to those who are suffering."

"O King Prasenjit, do not give too much importance and respect to the people around you. Do not get overly excited by the praises of others. Do not let yourself be content with external things, but always seek inner happiness. If you follow these principles, your good work will spread in every direction. As a King, always behave according to the Dhamma. We are all surrounded by high mountains of suffering and bad things in our lives."

"O King, good people behave according to the Dhamma teachings, they hate sensual pleasure and they condemn it, and they appreciate good things and they try to practice them in their lives. Truth cannot exist where there is lust, thirst and ignorance, just as birds cannot live on a burning tree. If a person is being praised as wise, but they do not have much knowledge of the Dhamma, they cannot be called a saint. One who knows these truths possesses wisdom. Dhamma knowledge is not reserved solely for ascetics, but can be practiced by anyone. Sometimes, an ordinary people can attain sainthood."

"O King, everyone has to experience the danger of lust. Everyone is ensnared in this vortex of lust. However, the Dhamma advises us to conduct ourselves in accordance with its teachings. We should all aspire to perform only good deeds, and it is necessary to critically evaluate our feelings and thoughts from time to time. We reap what we have sown. There are paths that lead from darkness to light and also from light to darkness."

"O King, one can demonstrate this superiority only by good conduct and the use of one's wisdom. All our happiness is fleeting, so concentrate on what is permanent in nature. Do not forget to perform your duty as a King."

King Prasenjit was greatly pleased to hear these noble words of Gautama Buddha. He promised the Buddha that he would follow the Dhamma teachings throughout his life as a king. After exchanging proper greetings, he took leave of the Buddha.

5. Piyajatika Sutta: Pain from loved one

The Buddha was once residing in Jetavana.

At that time, a householder's beloved child died. After his child's death, the householder felt no desire to work or eat. He was going to the cemetery and crying out,

"Where are you, my only child? Where is my only son, where has he gone?"

Then he went to the Buddha, bowed, and sat down beside him. After listening to his sad story, the Buddha said to him,

"Householder, you look like a person whose mind is not right, your mental faculties have become impaired."

"Yes, my friend, my mental faculties have become impaired because my beloved only child has passed away. Since his death, I have not felt like working or eating. I go to the cemetery and cry out,

"Where are you, my only child? Where are you, my only child?"

"That is quite true, householder! That is quite true, householder! Our loved ones are the source of our sorrow, lamentation, pain, sadness and trouble," the Buddha said.

Disagreeing with the Buddha's statement, he got up from his seat and left.

Now at that time, a number of gamblers were playing dice not far from the Jetavana. The householder came to them and told them what had happened. Gamblers listened to him and repeated the same words that the Buddha said to householder.

"It is quite true, householder! It is quite true, householder! Our loved ones are the source of our sorrow, lamentation, pain, sadness and trouble."

At last, that topic of discussion reached the royal compound.

Then King Prasenjit addressed Queen Mallika,

"Mallika, your ascetic Gautama said, our loved ones are the source of our sorrow, lamentation, pain, sadness and distress."

"If this is what the Buddha has said, O great king, it is so," said Queen Mallika.

King Prasenjit said,

"Mallika, you are like an obedient disciple, and you accept whatever the Buddha says."

"If this is what the Buddha has said, O great King, it is true, nothing else."

Then Queen Mallika said to the Brahmin Nadijangha,

"Please, Brahmin, go to the Buddha and bow your head at his feet in my name. After inquiring about him and his health, O Brahmin, may you ask the Buddha about his statement whether it is true or not that our loved ones are the source of suffering, lamentation, pain, sadness and distress?"

Remember well how the Buddha answers and tell me. Because the Buddha does not say anything that is not so."

"Yes, Madam," he replied.

He went to the Buddha and exchanged greetings with him. After greetings and polite conversation, he sat down on one side and said to the Buddha,

"Guru Gautama, Queen Mallika bows her head at your feet. She spoke about health and happiness, and she asked whether the Buddha made this statement: "Our loved ones are the source of suffering, lamentation, pain, sadness, and distress."

"That is right, Brahmin, that is right! Our loved ones are the source of our suffering, lamentation, pain, sadness and distress."

The Buddha said,

"Here is a way to understand how our loved ones are the source of our grief, lamentation, pain, sadness, and trouble."

The Buddha told about real events that happened in Shravasti.

"Once upon a time here in Shravasti, a woman's mother died. And because of this, she went mad and lost her mind. She went from street to street and crossroads to crossroads saying, has anybody seen my mother? Has anybody seen my mother?

This can be understood from another incident that once upon a time here in Shravasti, a woman's father... brother... sister... son... daughter... husband died. And because of this, she went mad and lost her mind. She went from street to street and crossroads to crossroads saying, has anybody seen my husband? Has anybody seen my father?

Once upon a time, right here in Sravasti, a woman lived with her husband's family. But her relatives wanted to divorce her from her husband and give her to someone else, which she did not want. So she told her husband about this. He cut her into two pieces and killed himself too, saying after death, we will be together. This is another way of understanding how our loved ones are the source of sorrow, lamentation, pain, sadness, and distress."

Then Nadijangha Brahmin, agreeing with the Buddha, got up from his place, went to Queen Mallika, and told her everything they had discussed.

Then Queen Mallika went to King Prasenjit and said to him, "Maharaj, what do you think? Do you love your daughter Princess Vajiri, Vasabha, and Prince Virudhak ?"

"Indeed, Mallika, it is true.

"What do you think, great king? If they die, decay, and perish, will sorrow, lamentation, pain, sadness, and distress arise in your mind?"

"Yes, indeed Mallika, if they die, decay, and perish, my life will perish. How can sorrow, lamentation, pain, sadness, and distress not arise in me?"

"This is what the Buddha was referring to when he said, our loved ones are the source of our sorrow, lamentation, pain, sadness, and distress."

"It is incredible, Mallika, it is amazing how far the Buddha sees with penetrating wisdom, it seems to me. Come Mallika, we can go to the Buddha."

Then King Prasenjit rose from his place, put his robe on one shoulder, and went to Jetavana to meet the Buddha.

King Prasenjit said,

"Guru Gautama, people say that you have advised people not to love. They say that the more you love, the more suffering and disappointment there will be. I believe life without love is meaningless. Please tell me the solution to this problem."

The Buddha looked at the king lovingly and said,

"Maharaj, many people will benefit from this question of yours. There are many types of love. Please try to understand the different aspects of love and the nature of love. Love is essential in life, but love based solely on sexuality, lust, physical attraction, and discrimination or prejudices is not ideal. is not true love. Love should be based on friendship (maitri) and compassion (karuna)."

"Generally, when we talk about love, we talk about the love that exists between father and child, husband and wife, members of a family, caste, or country. When our love is based on the belief in 'I' and 'mine', this type of love is based on attachment. In such love, we often fear losing the person, whether by accident or natural death. When the loss occurs in reality, it causes unbearable pain and sorrow."

"Love based on discrimination gives rise to prejudice. People either ignore or become hostile towards people other than their loved ones. Due to these attachments or prejudices, people become unhappy themselves and cause unhappiness in others."

The Buddha said, "All people are in need of love, friendship, and compassion. Friendship is the love that has the power to make others happy. Compassion is the love that enables the alleviation of others' suffering. Without friendship and compassion, life is meaningless and hollow. Friendship and compassion bring peace to life, making it full of joy and satisfaction. There is no hope of return in friendship and love. Friendship and compassion are not limited to one's relatives, parents, caste members or countrymen. When there is no discrimination, there is no attachment. It does not cause any sorrow or disappointment."

"As the ruler of a country, if you adopt the spirit of love, friendship, and compassion towards your subjects, then all your subjects will benefit. As a king, you should naturally love your family and your subjects, but your love and compassion should go beyond your family members and relatives because all the people of your kingdom are like your children."

The King said,

"But what about the youth of other kingdoms?"

"Who prevents you from loving the young men and women of other kingdoms as your own sons and daughters? Just because a ruler loves their subjects does not mean they should not love the subjects of other kingdoms. A ruler who governs with compassion does not have to rely on violent means."

Then King Prasenjit asked the Buddha,

"You say that love involves discrimination, expectations and attachments and these are the reasons for anxiety, suffering, and disappointment. Then how can I avoid anxiety and suffering when I love my children?"

Buddha said,

"For this, we have to recognize the true identity of our love. If our love is based on selfishness to assert our rights over others, then we cannot provide them with happiness and peace. On the contrary, our love will be a burden. For them, this love is a prison, which is worse than any burden."

"If the other person is not happy with our love, they will try to escape from it and gradually our love will bring anger and hatred. If you want your loved one to always be happy and joyful, then you must bear their sorrows and understand their aspirations. If you understand these things, then you will experience happiness and peace."

Buddha further explained:

"Everything in the world is temporary. One day or another, everything in the world will cease to exist. O King, one day, even your body will cease to exist. When we understand the temporary nature of this world, then we do not get troubled and our mind does not get troubled."

King Prasenjit was pleased by the Buddha's words. Queen Mallika and King Prasenjit stood up, bowed to the Buddha, and left the place.

That day, Queen Mallika and Princess Vaziri noticed a great change in the King's behavior. He looked unusually calm and full of loving-kindness.

6. Do not live like a miser

Once, Tathagata Buddha was staying at the Jetavana monastery. King Prasenjit came to the Buddha. After proper greetings, he took his seat and sat comfortably.

The Buddha saw him there in the hot summer, looking dejected and annoyed. So the Buddha asked about his purpose of coming there at such an odd time.

King Prasenjit of Kosal replied,

"Yes, Lord, you are right. A very wealthy man died in Shravasti without any legal heir. We went there to acquire his entire property because he had no one to take care of such a large property after him.

Lord, I really wonder why people behave like this. He was a wealthy man, but he did not use his wealth for his own welfare. He lived miserably, never wore good clothes, never ate nutritious food, and never gave generous donations to the needy or to the monks. He never rode in good chariots. He ended his life as a poor and destitute. He left behind eighty lakhs of gold coins and countless wealth."

The Buddha answered his question.

"O King, this is the fate of the wealth of a miser. Such a miser never enjoys his life; he never gives happiness to his family members; and he never gives charity generously to ascetics or needy persons. He spends his life like a poor and destitute person. His wealth is either taken away by kings, looted by robbers and thieves or destroyed by floods or fire."

"O King, collecting more wealth is like a large reservoir in a dense forest, whose water no one uses. Slowly that water evaporates, and the reservoir dries up. The life of a miser is also like this. A man who does not have greed for wealth is like a large reservoir near the village. All the villagers are using the water for cleaning, washing clothes, and drinking. Such water has great utility."

"The person who uses his wealth for his welfare and the happiness of his family members. He gives charity generously to the needy and ascetics; he gives food to the hungry and water to the thirsty. Such a person behaves according to the Dharma and enjoys his life well. A person completely immersed in greed and desire cannot distinguish between what is good and bad or between welfare and destruction. They behave like madmen and despite their wealth, they fail to earn the goodwill of people, relatives and family members in their lives."

On hearing this, King Prasenjit was very pleased and left the place, expressing his gratitude to the Buddha.

7. The fragrance is more powerful than the scent of flowers.

When the Buddha was residing in Shravasti, at that time one incident occurred. In the Kosal Kingdom, one wealthy merchant wanted to donate many precious ornaments like necklaces and all kinds of fine gems to King Prasenjt. The king was very pleased with this offer, however, he decided to give it to the public as a reward. He announced that all the men in the Kingdom should ask their wives to come out well-dressed, as he would give these fine ornaments to the most beautiful of them.

After the announcement, the wives immediately dressed themselves as best they could and appeared before the King, hoping to receive the precious items. The King noticed that only Queen Mallika was absent among them, so he asked his servant where she was.

Her attendant replied,

"Today, Queen Mallika is observing the eight precepts as taught by the Buddha. These eight prohibitive and fasting rules prohibit her from adorning herself with any makeup or jewelry, so she decided to stay in her room."

The King was very sad and sent his servant with a request to Queen Mallika to come out. When Queen Mallika finally appeared, wearing her simple attire without any decorations, and she had not applied any cosmetics, yet her whole body was radiant and looked even more dignified and majestic than usual.

The King was very surprised, and he asked Queen Mallika, "What is it that makes you look so different from the rest here?"

Queen Mallika replied,

"Because I have eliminated all the accumulated negative karma in my life and I have restrained myself from strong craving and attachment to everything. Furthermore, I understood that life is brief and temporary. If we do not work hard at developing good karma, it will be very easy for us to fall into the evil path. Therefore, I now take and follow the eight precepts (Ashtashila) every month to give up my strong greed and desires, and follow the Buddha's teachings. With these practices, I hope I will be able to obtain the benefits of the Dhamma."

The King was very pleased with her explanation and decided to give Queen Mallika the precious jewels. However, Queen Mallika replied,

"Today I am observing the eight precepts, and therefore it would not be appropriate for me to wear these jewels. Please, give it to someone else."

The King said,

"My intention is to award these precious items to the most beautiful woman here, and among them you are the most beautiful, charming and dignified. Moreover, by following the eight precepts (eight rules) of the Buddha, your mind is pure, free from afflictions. This makes people love and respect you. If you do not accept this gift, what can I possibly do?"

Queen Mallika replied,

"Your Majesty, please come with me, and we will go and offer these jewels to the Buddha and his Sangha."

King Prasenjit and Queen Mallika, accompanied by top ministers, went to the Jetavana monastery where the Buddha was staying.

After prostrating before the Buddha, the King took the jewels in his hand and told the Buddha,

"Queen Mallika, by following the eight precepts (ashta-sila), is unable to wear these jewels. Because her mind is in a state of detachment. Therefore, she humbly refuses this precious gift that I gave her. Therefore, we have come here especially to offer you this treasure, and I hope you will kindly accept it."

The King also asked,

"Is there any merit in receiving and observing the eight precepts (ashta-shila) and believing in the Dharma?"

The Buddha then provided a few lines of advice to all those present, the meaning of which is as follows:

"Even the wonderful fragrance of the most fragrant sandalwood or lotus flower in the world will still be much weaker than the fragrance coming from a person who follows the eight precepts (ashta-shila). If one's action can remain in accordance with the principles and maintain good moral conduct, that person will be bound to rid himself of all his vices and errors, thus freeing himself or herself from all troubles as well as all sufferings. The eight prohibitions and vows are also called the eight precepts or eight shila (precepts). These precepts encourage the laity to temporarily experience the monastic life. The practitioner should leave their family for one day and one night, live with the Sangha to learn the monastic life and refrain from killing, stealing, sexual misconduct, lying, taking intoxicants, wearing garlands, ornaments and perfumes, dancing, singing, playing music, sitting or lying on a lavish seat or bed, and not eating after noon."

The Buddha continued,

"The merits gained by upholding these precepts are vast and long-lasting, and as a result, practitioners will gain a good reputation and receive high respect from their peers. Even if you take all the treasures of the entire world and give them away as offerings, all the merit you gain would not be as great as what Queen Mallika gained from observing the precepts in a single day. Following the eight precepts can help free oneself from suffering, thereby attaining nirvana. Merits of this kind cannot be compared to worldly merits."

After the Buddha spoke, everyone was very pleased and followed the Buddha's instructions with resolve, and decided to practice the Dhamma.

8. Sattajatila Sutta - Seven Matted Ascetics

The Buddha explains how to evaluate a person's character.

Once, the Buddha was staying at the Pubbarama monastery built by Visakha, the King Prasenjit went to the Buddha, bowed respectfully, sat down on one side and said to him.

King Prasenjit told the Buddha the following incident:

King Prasenjit told the Buddha that he met seven matted, naked ascetics. Their armpits and bodies were hairy, and their nails were long; and they carried their belongings on poles hanging over their shoulders.

When I saw these seven ascetics, I rose from my seat, put my robe over my shoulder, put my right knee on the ground, raised my joined palms toward the seven ascetics, and pronounced their names three times: "Respected ascetics, I am King Prasenjit, I am King Prasenjit, I am King Prasenjit. However, the seven ascetics left without saying anything."

"It seems that, among the ascetics I just met, some are enlightened and some are practicing the path of enlightenment."

In answer to his question, the Buddha said, "Great King, as a common man the king enjoys worldly pleasures, living at home with wives and children, using various perfumes, adorning the body with ornaments and flowers, using makeup and using gold and wealth. It is difficult to know who is enlightened or who is on the path to enlightenment."

"Oh! Majesty, you can get to know a person's ethics by living with them. But only after a long time, not casually; only when paying attention, not when inattentive; and only by the wise, not the witless. You can get to know a person's purity by dealing with them. You can get to know a person's resilience in times of trouble. You can get to know a person's wisdom by discussion. But only after a long time, not casually; only when paying attention, not when inattentive. We can evaluate a person only by being wise, not by being foolish."

King Prasenjit said,

"It is unbelievable, it is amazing, how beautifully you have described this incident to me. Those ascetics are my spies and secret agents, returning after gathering intelligence in various provinces. First, they go incognito, and then they report to me. Soon, they will wash off the dust, take a bath, apply perfume, comb their hair and beard, and dress themselves neatly. Then, they will entertain themselves surrounded by worldly pleasures."

Then, on that occasion, the Buddha spoke these verses in connection with this incident.

"It's not easy to know a man by his appearance.
You shouldn't trust them at first sight.
Undisciplined people live in this world,
disguised as the disciplined.

Like a fake earring made of silver,
like a copper penny coated with gold,
they live hidden in the world,
corrupt inside but impressive outside."

King Prasenjit became very happy on hearing these verses, and after proper salutation, he left the place.

9. The True Lion Roar of Queen Srimala

Once, the Buddha was residing in the Jetavana. At that time, King Prasenjit and Queen Malikā had an initial realization of the Dhamma. They said to each other, "Our daughter Srimala is kind, intelligent, and learned. She is quick to understand the profound Dhamma of the Tathagata, there will be no doubt about that. Now, we must send a messenger to summon her here."

Soon after this decision was made, the King and Queen wrote a letter to Srimala describing the true merits of the Tathagata and sent the messenger Chandra to deliver it to Ayodhya.

Queen Srimala received the letter with reverence and joy. Srimala traveled from Ayodhya to Sravasti to meet the Buddha, in accordance with her parents' request.

When Srimala met the Buddha, he told her that she had practiced the Dharma for a long time, and her wisdom and simplicity were subtle and profound.

Queen Srimala then said to the Buddha,

"World honoured Tathagata Buddha, I wish to explain the broad meaning of true Dhamma. Queen Srimala said that embracing true Dhamma is nothing but embracing the paramitās, and the paramitās are nothing but embracing the true Dhamma."

Srimaala further said,

"Purify their own verbal, physical and mental actions and conduct themselves with dignity. Thus, they bring those beings to maturity according to their inclinations. They establish them firmly in the true Dhamma. This is called the paramita of discipline.

Those sentient beings can mature best by patience, free from ill will, rebuke, insult, resentment, slander, libel, annoyance, and persecution. Thus, they bring those beings to maturity according to their inclinations; this is called the paramita of patience.

Those sentient beings do not have laziness or negative mindsets, but show great aspiration and utmost enthusiasm, whether walking, standing, sitting, or lying down. Thus, they bring those beings to maturity according to their inclinations; this is called the paramita of vigor or virya.

Those sentient beings who are not distracted and achieve right mindfulness and remembrance with their inclination, that is called the paramita of mindfulness.

Those sentient beings who can mature with wisdom and who can ask questions about the Dhamma to benefit from it, who embrace the Dhamma without ceasing to explain all the doctrines, all the sciences, all the techniques, until they fully understand what is the ultimate, are called the paramita of wisdom."

The Buddha said to Srimala,

"Now you should embrace and expand the true Dhamma, which I taught."

Queen Srimala said;

"There are two kinds of defilement: inherent and active defilement.

The inherent defilements are four in number, what are they?

Attachment to particular viewpoints, attachment to desire, attachment to form, and craving for existence. These four inherent defilements can generate active defilements. Active defilements arise moment by moment along with the mind.

These four defilements are powerful. Yet, compared with them, the inherent defilement of ignorance is so much more powerful, and this difference is indescribable by either figures or analogies. The defilement of ignorance is more powerful than the craving for existence. Only through knowledge can all defilements be eradicated. Once the defilement of inherent ignorance is cut off, all these defilements will be cut off together.

Queen Srimala continued, "I can explain the great meaning in detail." The Buddha said, "Explain the great meaning."

Good men and women who practice the true Dhamma give their bodies, lives, and possessions for the true Dharma. They will attain inexhaustible, imperishable, perfect attainments, unimaginable merits and splendid virtues, and will be respected and served by other beings."

Queen Srimala said,

"O Venerable Tathagata Buddha, when the true Dhamma is on the verge of extinction, the monks, nuns, lay people will gather in different groups, form different factions, and dispute with each other. At that time, good men and women who cherish and embrace the true Dhamma, without malice or deceit, will join the good faction."

The Buddha praised her level of understanding of the true Dhamma.

10. Everything in nature is perishable.

The news of Queen Mallika's death reached King Prasenjit while he was listening to the Buddha's sermon at Jetavana. It appeared that Mallika died suddenly. He suddenly experienced great shock and grief after hearing the sad news of Queen Mallika's death. The Buddha also came to know the news of Queen Mallika's death.

The Buddha tried to console King Prasenjit by saying,

"All beings are perishable; they end with death. All pots made by a potter, whether baked or unbaked, are breakable; they break eventually. They are prone to breakage. Pain and sorrow cannot shake the wise person who understands the reality of nature: that all things born will one day die. Do not grieve, do not lament as there is no benefit in grieving."

Buddha further said in a consoling tone,

"O King, everyone of us has the same feeling that no member of my family should die, he should not suffer, everything should remain the same. O King, we have to accept the reality of nature that everything is changing, dying, and perishing every moment. O King, those who are ignorant of the reality of nature express sorrow at the suffering and pain caused to themselves and their relatives. Such people cause more trouble to the body and become weak. O King, we will all die one day. So instead of cursing and lamenting, we need to face the situation bravely and adopt this golden principle in our lives."

Buddha told him about the inevitability of old age and death, one can reduce one's suffering by understanding the impermanence of everything that comes into existence. Instead of mourning the death of Queen Mallika, we should accept her good qualities, deeds and adopt them in our lives.

11. Ideal Administrative System

During the winter season, Queen Mallika died, and King Prasenjit was very sad, unhappy, and depressed due to her death. The Queen was his great advisor. They had spent more than 40 years of married life. King Prasenjit came to Buddha to console himself. He started spending more time with Buddha and also started practicing meditation. Buddha reminded King Prasenjit to do the following things that would make others happy:

- Improve the judiciary system and financial health of the state.
- Giving severe punishments to criminals like the death penalty or putting them in prisons does not help in reducing crimes in the state, because crime is often a result of hunger and helplessness.
- A strong financial system should be implemented to provide security to the people and society as a whole.
- Provide grains, seeds, fertilizers, and other resources to farmers to do farming until their condition improves.
- Provide loans to small businessmen.

- The government should provide relief to those unable to work and offer tax relief to low-income people.
- Allow people the freedom to conduct their business according to their own choices.
- For those who want to do business and need skills, the state should arrange for skill training.
- The right financial system should be based on people's participation.

King Prasenjit listened to the Buddha very carefully and promised to implement these suggestions.

After proper greetings, King Prasenjit left from Jetavana.

II: To Anathapindika

1. Four Eternal Pleasures

Whenever the Buddha was staying in Jetavana, Anathapindika used to visit the Buddha twice a day. He tried to attend each of the Buddha's Dhamma sermons. Anathapindika was a soft-spoken person. Whenever Anathapindika came to the Buddha, after proper greetings, he used to sit quietly on one side. He would wait to hear the sermon. If the Buddha did not speak anything on Dhamma, he would start the discussion with incidents from his life.

Anathapindika asked the Buddha what the four things are that give happiness after giving charity.

The Buddha said,

"The four requisites for bhikkhus are food, clothing, shelter and medicine, which give happiness to those who gives these as a donation to bhikkhus."

What are the four things that give happiness to householders?

The Buddha said,

"The joy of owning something, the joy of possessing wealth, the joy of being free from any kind of debt, the joy of being free from any kind of blemish."

The Buddha explained each aspect further:

He said,

"It gives immense pleasure when someone possesses something of his own. Anyone who has earned wealth with great effort and in the right way, the owner of wealth takes pleasure simply by realizing that his wealth has been earned with great effort and in a legitimate way. This gives him immense satisfaction. He takes pleasure in being free from any kind of debt. One who is free from any bad karma done by the body, by speaking and by thinking evil, he feels the joy of living an untainted life."

These are the four eternal pleasures that any householder can enjoy.

2. Why did she call me brother?

Anathapindika had a daughter named Sumna. She used to help her father in his daily religious activities. Naturally, Anathapindika was very happy with his daughter. But it is said that who has control over time.

Once Sumna fell seriously ill. Despite extensive treatment, she could not recover and passed away. Before her death, she addressed her father as 'Brother'. Anathapindika was very sad at the death of his daughter. But he was even more saddened by the thought that before dying, his daughter had called him 'Brother'. He felt that before dying, his daughter had lost her mental balance. He was unable to understand how this happened?

With a heavy heart, he went to Buddha and bowed to him and sat in front of him. Seeing his expressions, Buddha asked him why he was looking so upset? Then Anathapindika told him the reason.

After listening to his problem, Buddha explained to him, 'Anathapindika, you need not to worry. Your daughter did not lose her mental balance. You are a Sotapanna and she was a Sakridagami. Thus, she was one step ahead of you on the spiritual ladder. Therefore, if she addressed you as "Brother, you should not feel bad about it."

After listening to this, Anathapindika understood the matter and his sorrow went away.

3. Seven types of wives

When the Buddha was staying in the Jetavana in Shravasti, Anathapindika came to the Buddha to invite him and his Sangha for lunch. Upon his request, the next day, the Buddha along with his Sangha went to Anathapindika's house for lunch as per the invitation. When they reached there, they saw some chaotic scenes and situations inside the house, with noise of some screaming and sounds of utensils falling down and also coming from the inside.

The Buddha inquired about this chaotic situation. Anathapindika expressed regret and said that his daughter-in-law named Sujata is from a rich family and moreover, she does not have a sense of civilized behavior within the family. As stated, since she is arrogant, she becomes angry with everyone in the family. O Lord, I have prepared a meal for you.

After the meal was finished, the Buddha requested all the family member to come and listen. When all the family members gathered, he asked Sujata,

"O my daughter Sujata, do you know how many kinds of wives there are and what kind of wife are you?"

She admitted her lack of knowledge on the subject and asked the Buddha to tell her the types of wives.

The Buddha agreed to her request and began his sermon. He said, "There are seven kinds of wives."

- First, a wife whose mind is malicious and is unfaithful in marriage, abandons her husband, has improper relations with other men because she is captivated by their wealth or beauty and disdains her husband. She is attracted to and affectionate towards others. The Tathagata considers such a wife to be like a murderer.
- The second type of wife is one who does not properly manage the family's finances; instead, she squanders the lawful property earned by her husband. The Tathagata deems such a wife similar to a robber and a thief.

- The third type of wife is one who is proud of her wealth, property, beauty, and talents and is lazy regardless of the circumstances. She does not speak lovingly and does not get along well with her husband. But she only knows how to speak in a rude manner. And she dominates her husband. Such a wife is considered like a master.
- The fourth type of wife is one who likes to take care of her husband and his family members. She assists her husband and his family. She knows how to preserve and grow her husband's property, like a mother who fully cares for her family and children. Such a wife is considered akin to a mother.
- The fifth type of wife is one who is meek, dignified, humble, and knows how to pamper her husband like a brother in the family. Such a wife is said to be like a sister.
- The sixth type of wife is always friendly, cordial, happy, and harmonious with her husband, like meeting a close friend one has not met for a long time. She is always virtuous and loyal to her husband. Such a wife is said to be like a friend.
- The seventh type of wife is always flexible, does not get angry, and does not show a rude or forceful attitude even when her husband behaves unkindly. On the contrary, she also knows how to advise her husband skillfully and win his heart. Such a wife is like a servant.

After listening to the seven types of wives as described by the Buddha, Sujata expressed her gratitude to the Buddha for his valuable guidance. Sujata vowed that she would try to become an ideal wife and an ideal daughter-in-law.

After expressing deep gratitude, the Buddha and his Sangha left the house of Anathapinaka.

4. Dhamma Teachings at the Time of Anāthapindika's Death

The householder Anāthapindika who had invited the Buddha to Shravasti, had donated the Jetavana to the Buddha and his Sangha. He became seriously ill for the third time and had very intense pain that was getting worse and was not relieved. Anāthapindika then asked the Venerable Sariputta and the Venerable Ananda for help. When the

Venerable Sariputta saw him, he knew that Anāthapindika was near death, and he gave him the following Dhamma teachings.

Sariputta told Anāthapindika that he should practice freeing himself from clinging to the six sense objects and not attach his thoughts to them; secondly, he should practice freeing himself from dependence on the six sense objects and not attach his thoughts to them. Third, he must stop clinging to the six senses and the six sense objects, as well as to the connecting link between the six sense contacts, the six emotions, the six elements, the five aggregates:*form* (rupa -the material image or impression); *sensations* (vedana- feelings received from form); *perceptions* (samjna- recognition, labels or ideas; mental activity or formations); and *sankhara* (influences of the past); *discernment* (vijnana-awareness or understanding) and the four formless worlds (the realm of boundless empty space, the realm of boundless consciousness, the realm of nothingness, and the realm of no thought), detach from what is in the mind. Detach from what he has heard, thought, considered and examined.

Anāthapiṇḍika listened attentively and understood to these detailed instructions given by Sāriputta. He was already practicing in the same way as Venerable Sāriputta had instructed him.

Then the Venerable Sariputta said, "O Anathapindika, this profound teaching can only be understood by monks, not ordinary disciples.

Anathapindika replied,

"Venerable Sariputta, such talks on the Dhamma should also be given to lay disciples. The layperson is a little confused, with a little dust in their eye. If they do not hear such teachings, they will be lost, and they will never become wise. If they hear such profound teachings, few people will understand anything."

Sariputta replied,

"Anāthapindika, as a disciple who had the fruit of stream-entry, had the five aggregates of the transitory nature and he himself expressed the fact that he knew the three characteristics of existence: *impermanence, suffering, and non-self.* But there is a great difference between simply hearing these talks and contemplating them versus actually practicing and applying their relevance to oneself. In this difference lies the essential difference between the way the Buddha taught to householders and the way he taught to monks."

Having thus given the Dhamma discourse to Anāthapindika, Venerable Sariputta and Venerable Ananda departed. Soon after, the householder Anāthapindika died peacefully.

IV. To Visakha

1. Love gives rise to suffering

On one occasion, when the Buddha was residing at the Pubbarama Monastery, Visakha went to the Buddha in the middle of the day, wearing wet clothes, disheveled and with tears in her eyes. When the Buddha asked her why she was upset, she told him that her beloved granddaughter had died suddenly.

The Buddha asked her if she wanted grandchildren equal to the number of citizens of Sravasti. When she said yes, the Buddha said that many people were dying in Shravasti every day and would she come to the Buddha all the time to express her sorrow for all those people in the same state of suffering. The Buddha told her that everything is impermanent in nature. We become sad due to our intense attachment to a particular place, person or object. The amount of our suffering and unhappiness depends on the level of our attachment to that person.

The Buddha continued:

"Love gives rise to suffering.

Love creates fear.

For one who is free from love,

there is no suffering, because there is no fear."

2. Women should possess these qualities.

While staying at Pubbarama Monastery, the Buddha gave another discourse to Visakha. She went to the Buddha on a full moon day to seek his blessings and advice, following the eight precepts of Buddhist ethics. Visakha asked the Buddha what qualities will help a woman to be happy and successful in this life.

Answering the question raised by Visakha, the Buddha said,

- A woman does her work well.
- She manages servants well.
- She respects her husband, other family members, and others.
- She protects her wealth.

V. To Bhukkhu Sangha.

1. For Whom Dhamma is

In the presence of the Buddha, once at Shravasti, Bhante Aniruddha gave a Dhamma discourse in which he stated for whom the Dhamma teachings are intended. Bhante Aniruddha gave eight reflections on the Dhamma for monks, which are:

- The Dhamma is intended for those who are contented and do not desire much in their lives, not for those who are always dissatisfied.
- The Dhamma is intended for those who prefer solitude, not for those who enjoy the company of others.
- The Dhamma is for energetic people, not for indolent people.
- The Dhamma is intended for the alert-minded, not the careless.
- The Dhamma is intended for the concentrated mind, not the distracted mind.
- This Dhamma is intended for the wise, not for the foolish.
- This Dhamma is intended for those who find pleasure in Nirvana, not for those who find pleasure in worldliness (conceit, craving, and wrong view).

2. Seven factors that earn respect and honor for monks:

- Having no desire for gain.
- Not seeking honor and being indifferent to public attention.
- Being ashamed of doing evil.
- Being afraid of doing evil.

- Having few wants and needs, and
- Having the right view.

3 Bhikkhus should not go to such places

Bhikkhus should not visit or stay in the residence of laypeople where the following shortcomings are found in some people.

- Where bhikkhus are not welcomed or signs of welcome are not shown, and proper seating arrangements have not been made for bhikkhus. Bhikkhus should not go to such a place.
- Where alms are kept hidden, very little alms or donations are given when there is a possibility of more such alms or donations, where poor quality alms are given even when better alms are available, and where donations are given in a disrespectful manner.
- Where laypeople do not come to bhikkhus to listen to the Dhamma, and where little interest is shown in the explanation of the Dhamma.

4. Impurities of the Mind

- Greed and excessive greed are impurities of the mind.
- Ill will is an impurity of the mind.
- Anger is an impurity of the mind.
- Revenge is an impurity of the mind.
- Slander is the filth of the mind.
- Domineering is an impurity of the mind.
- Jealousy is an impurity of the mind.
- Stinginess is an impurity of the mind.
- Cheating is an impurity of the mind.
- Stubbornness is an impurity of the mind.
- Presumption is an impurity of the mind.
- Egoism is an impurity of the mind.
- Carelessness is an impurity of the mind.

Being clearly aware that these are impurities of the mind, Bhikkhus should strive to overcome them.

5. Live in the present.

In Jetavana, a Bhikhu named Thera never spoke to anyone. He walked alone and did not violate any rules. However, he did not live in harmony with the rest of the Bhikkhu community. Other Bhikkhu began to call him a recluse.

The Buddha came to know of this. The next day, after preaching the Dhamma, the Buddha called Bhante Thera and asked,

"Is it true that you live alone and avoid contact with other Bhikkhu?"

The senior Bhikkhu Thera replied,

"That is true, Bodhisattva. You are the one who tells us to be self-reliant and practice alone."

In this regard, the Buddha while addressing the Bhikkhu Sangha, said,

"What is real self-reliance? A self-reliant person is one who lives in a conscious state. He knows what is happening in the present moment. He knows what is happening to his body, emotions, and mind and he knows how to experience or perceive all the elements in the present moment. He neither runs after the past nor does he let himself get caught in the web of the future. Because the past is over and the future has not yet come. Whatever is there in life, we have to live in the present. If we lose the present, we lose life. Living in the present and enjoying the present moment is the best way to live alone."

Buddha further said,

"Bhikkhus, what is the meaning of digging into the past? It means that you think about what you were in the past, whom you were attracted to at that time, what kind of happy, sad experiences you had. Such thoughts entangle you in the past. Bhikkhus, what does it mean to fall into the trap of future delusion? When you get lost in thoughts of the future? You think and hope, fear or worry about the future. You speculate about what you will look like in the future, what you will be like, what your feelings will be and whether you will be happy or sad. All these thoughts trap you in the trap of future delusion."

"Bhikkhus, living in the present keeps us in touch with life and helps us to understand life attentively. If you do not have direct contact with life, you will not be able to understand deeply what is happening in the present, and you will lose your mental awareness and you will not be truly living in the present.

Bhikkhus, when we really know the present moment, we can be alone even in a crowd. If a person is sitting alone in a forest and the past or the future surrounds them, they are not really alone."

The Buddha neither praised nor criticized Bhante Thera, but it was evident that the Bhikkhu was now more clear about the meaning and difference between self-reliance and solitude.

6. Do not dwell on the past and do not dream of the future

Once Tathagat Buddha was residing in the Jetavana Vaihara, some bhikkhus came to visit the Buddha from the Pubbarama Vihara.

After paying proper obeisance to the Buddha, the Bhikkhus told the Buddha that the newly appointed Bhante Shraddhankara always remembers his past, and Bhante Siddhapala is more concerned about attaining Nirvana. Therefore, these two bhikkhus are unable to concentrate on their vipassana meditation practice. However, these two bhikkhus are highly disciplined, following every instruction of the Sangha.

The Buddha asked them to join the evening Dhamma meeting with all the bhikkhus including Shraddhankara and Siddhapala.

When the Bhikkhus, along with the other two Bhikkhus, gathered for the evening Dhamma meeting, the Buddha resumed the Dhamma discourse.

"O Bhante, listen carefully."

"Bhante, do not be too sad remembering your past and do not be too anxious about your golden future. Because the past is gone, and the future is yet to come. Please try to see and enjoy the present moments in life, but without craving, attachment or getting angry due to hatred or ill will. You observe your present moment without any attachment through Vipassana.

Bhikkhus, do not pay much attention to the past, and do not worry about whatever happened in the past, whether it was bad or good. Similarly, don't worry too much about your future, which is yet to come. Think deeply and carefully about the present moment, and do your best in this present moment. Whatever you have to do, do it today, because we don't know anything about the future. Anything can happen, like an earthquake, sudden death or an attack by the enemy, etc. Those who are alert and careful about the present moments enjoy life.

A person who does not spend their present moment in hatred, anger, or craving experiences peace in life by embracing the Dhamma."

"Do not dwell on the past or think about it like: I was very beautiful, attractive, energetic, wealthy, or poor, strong or weak. People who think about the future, like I will become the president of a powerful state, I will be beautiful, attractive, and energetic, I will have enough money to enjoy, I will have a beautiful life partner, sometimes people do not always enjoy their life."

"O Bhante, always practice Dhamma, try to associate with wise people, try to understand the impermanent nature of everything in this world, and do not surrender yourself to any kind of craving, attachment or hatred."

Hearing this sermon of the Buddha, two monks, Shraddhankar and Siddhapala, realized their mistakes. All the monks thanked the Buddha and left.

6. Enjoy the present

Once the Buddha was staying in Jetavana, there he addressed the assembly of monks by saying;

"Bhante, listen carefully and pay attention to it."

The Buddha continued:

"Do not wander in the past, do not yearn for the future. The past has disappeared, and the future has not come.

Only the present event exists. One must see it insightfully every moment and firmly enter it, always unwavering, always undefeated.

Because who knows, tomorrow death may come? There is no bargaining with mighty death.

To dwell in this way, always striving day and night, never slacking off, is the true commitment to ultimate peace.

Bhikkhus, how does one wander in the past, thinking that in the past, I had such a physical form? One feels happy thinking, I also had such perceptions in the past. One may feel happy reminiscing about one's past physical form. One feels happy thinking, I had such a consciousness in the past. Thus, one gets lost in the past. One should not take pleasure in the past by thinking about the past.

Now, if one is longing for the future, one wonders if one will get such a body in the future? One takes pleasure in thinking, can I get such perceptions in the future? One feels happy thinking, will I get such a material structure in the future? One feels happy thinking will I get such a consciousness in the future. Bhante, one should not be pleased at events that will happen in the future."

The Buddha further said,

"Be in the present, live in the present, enjoy the present. Avoid yearning for the future, as the past has vanished, and the future is yet to arrive. The present is all that exists; one must perceive it with clarity every moment, live in the present, remain unwavered, and be undefeated. Work must be done today, without waiting for the future; who knows, death may come tomorrow. There is no compromise with that mighty death."

"Thus enjoying, always striving, day and night, never slacking off. This is called the only commitment by the great Bhante Buddha, the ultimate peace lover."

8. Always practice awareness.

On one occasion, the Buddha was staying at the Jetavana monastery with many great disciples, such as Sariputta, Maha Moggallana, Maha Kasyapa, Maha Kakkana, Maha Kothita, Maha Kappina, Maha Kunda, Revata, Aniruddha, Ananda, and others. It was a full-moon night on the fifteenth Uposatha day at Pubbarama monastery, and the Buddha was seated in the open air surrounded by a group of Bhikkhus.

Some of them were teaching ten Bhikkhus, some twenty Bhikkhus, some thirty Bhikkhus, some forty Bhikkhus.

Surveying the community of Bhikkhus, the Buddha addressed them:

"Bhikkhus, I am satisfied with this practice. You need to awaken with even more intense determination to attain the unattainable.

Bhikkhus, one must always practice awareness. For this, practice your breathing in and out. Wherever you are, whether in the forest, in the shade of a tree or in an empty building, sit with your legs crossed, your body erect. When you take a deep breath, understand that you are taking a deep breath. When you take a shallow breath, understand that you are taking a shallow breath; when you breathe out, understand that you are breathing out.

Always be aware and breathe in with sensitivity to the whole body, and breathe out with sensitivity to the whole body.

Breathe in with sensitivity to joy. On any occasion, be aware of your breathing and feel the sensation of inhaling and exhaling. While meditating, feel that I am breathing less, be sensitive to the whole body. At that moment, the Bhikkhu's mind is centered in the body and in itself - enthusiastic, alert, and there is no greed, craving or aversion in the mind."

The Buddha further said,

"I tell you, Bhikkhus, that this is to observe with equanimity the coming and going of the breath. Bhikkhus, on any occasion, one is to remain centered on the body and in oneself - enthusiastic, alert, and steady on that occasion, abandoning greed and distress in the context of the mind-world.

By thus fixing the mind, one examines, analyzes and discerns that quality with discernment. When one examines and analyzes in this way, the analysis of qualities as a factor for awakening is awakened.

When the mind of one who is spontaneous - his body is quiet - becomes concentrated, concentration as a factor for awakening is awakened. He develops it, and for him it reaches the culmination of its development.

He carefully observes the mind, thus concentrating with equanimity. When he carefully concentrates the mind with equanimity, equanimity as a factor for awareness is awakened. He develops it, and for him it reaches the culmination of its development."

9. Discourse on breathing in and out

The Buddha was staying in the Pubbarama Monastery with Sariputra, Maha Moggallana, Maha Kassapa, Maha Kaccana, Maha Kothita, Maha Kapina, Maha Kunda, Anuruddha, Revata, Ananda, and other learned senior disciples. At that time, the elder Bhikkhus were advising and instructing the novices. One elderly Bhikkhu advised ten novices, another advised twenty novices, another thirty, and then forty novices. The novices, being advised and instructed by the elder Bhikkhus, also attained specific levels that had never been attained before. On that full moon night, the Buddha was sitting outside in the moonlight in the presence of the community of Bhikkhus.

The Buddha observed the silent community of Bhikkhus and addressed them,

"Bhikkhus, I am happy to see the progress of learning by Bhikkhus. Therefore, the bhikkhus made great efforts to attain that which has not been attained and to realize that which has not yet been realized. Bhikkhus, this assembly is devoid of idle talk, devoid of empty chatter, and established in pure essence. Such an assembly is worthy of respect, worthy of hospitality, worthy of offerings and reverential salutations, and to the world, it becomes an incomparable field of merit. In this assembly, there are worthy people who have destroyed desires, have lived holy lives, have done what should be done, have come to the highest good, have destroyed the bondage of 'being.' In this assembly, there are bhikkhus who have overcome the bondage of the sensual world in this life. In this assembly, there are bhikkhus who have overcome the three fetters of greed, hatred, and delusion.

In this assembly, there are bhikkhus who are practicing the Noble Eightfold Path. In this assembly, there are bhikkhus who are inspired to cultivate loving-kindness. In this assembly, there are bhikkhus inspired to develop compassion. In this assembly, there are bhikkhus inspired to develop inner joy. In this assembly, there are bhikkhus inspired to develop equanimity. In this assembly, there are bhikkhus who are committed to not developing any sense of hatred. In this assembly, there are bhikkhus who are cultivating the understanding of impermanence. In this assembly, there are bhikkhus who are cultivating the awareness of their inhalations and exhalations. Bhikkhus, the practice of mindful breathing yields beneficial outcomes.

How does this bring more results? The Bhikkhu, in the forest or under a tree or inside an empty house, should sit cross-legged, keeping the body erect to establish meditation. When the bhikkhu takes a long breath in meditation, he is aware that he is taking a long breath. When he takes short breath, he is aware that he is taking short breath.

I feel a sense of pleasure when I inhale. I feel a sense of pleasure when I exhale. I experience a sense of pleasantness as I breathe in and out. I am experiencing the mental determination with which I breathe in. I breathe in and out with a joyful mind. I breathe in and out with a focused mind. With a calm mind, I breathe in and breathe out. Reflecting on impermanence, I breathe in and out. Reflecting on equanimity (upekshābhāva), I breathe in and out. Reflecting on cessation, I breathe in and out. The process of breathing in and out, developed in this way, brings much fruit and great benefit.

Bhikkhus, having developed and practiced breathing in and out in this way, the four stages of meditation have been mastered. At such times, one remains mindful of letting go of greed and displeasure towards samsara. Bhikkhus, I say that inhaling and exhaling are characteristics of the body. At such times, the bhikkhu continues to reflect on enthusiasm in the body to remain mindful and aware, letting go of greed and displeasure towards samsara. Bhikkhus, I say that inhaling and exhaling is a characteristic of the emotions when they are meditated upon. So, bhikkhus, at such times, the bhikkhu reflects on feelings to be mindful of letting go of greed and aversion for the world.

Bhikkhus, when he is experiencing the mental state, he inhales and exhales. In this state, he inhales and exhales with a happy mind.

When the bhikkhu is reflecting on impermanence, he feels he breathes in and out, and he trains himself to reflect on detachment, which reflects cessation. He is reflecting on letting go. He wisely acts to let go of whatever greed and displeasure there is in the world and takes possession of it. At such times, the bhikkhu adheres to reflecting on the thoughts in the teaching, being mindful of letting go of greed and aversion for the world. Bhikkhus, when developed and built up in this way, the four foundations of mindfulness are complete.

How do the four stages of mindfulness develop? At this stage, the bhikkhu continues to reflect on the body by being conscious and aware to overcome greed and aversion towards the world, and their mindfulness is established without forgetting. At the time mindfulness is established, the enlightenment factor of mindfulness is established for the bhikkhu. At this stage, the bhikkhu develops and perfects the enlightenment factor of mindfulness. He continues to search for a solution by carefully examining those thoughts. When the bhikkhu carefully examines the teaching to find a solution, they develop the enlightenment factor to examine the teaching and perfect it. When those thoughts are examined wisely with conscious effort to directly find a solution, the enlightenment factor of effort is established for the bhikkhu. At that time, the bhikkhu develops and perfects the enlightenment factor of effort. Non-physical bliss arises from this conscious effort. When this immaterial bliss arises, the bhikkhu is established in the enlightenment factor of joy, and it becomes complete. When the mind is happy, the body is also happy. When the mind and body are satisfied, the enlightenment factor of calmness is established in the bhikkhu, and with development, it becomes complete. When the body is happy, the mind is concentrated. At that time, the bhikkhu is established in the enlightenment factor of concentration, and with development, it becomes complete. The bhikkhu examines the concentrated mind deeply. At that time, the bhikkhu is established in the enlightenment factor of equanimity, and with this development, it becomes complete.

When the bhikkhu develops and perfects the enlightenment factor of mindfulness, they examine those thoughts carefully and wisely search for solutions. Immaterial bliss arises from awakened effort."

All the assembled bhikkhus expressed their heartfelt gratitude to the Buddha, and then they left.

10. Sallekha Sutta: Discourse on Effort

Once, the Buddha was living in Jetavana. Then, one evening, the respected Maha-Kunda rose from the meditation solitude and went to the Buddha. After bowing to him, he sat on one side and spoke to the Buddha like this:

"Respected sir, these various views arise in the world regarding self-principles or world-principles. Can a bhikkhu renounce such ideas that only occur at the beginning of their thinking?"

The Buddha explained to Mahakund,

"O Mahakund, you need to understand the following eight mental conditions arising during meditation (vipassana) regarding self-principles and world-principles.

It may be that someone has withdrawn from the senses, and once they are withdrawn from the senses, the absorption which is born from disinterest (detachment, equanimity). With prudent thinking and filled with enthusiasm and happiness, they can then think; they are stable in calmness (a tranquil state of mind). The person with mental discipline does not call it a calmness (tranquil state of mind), but they call it there and now with ease.

In the second phase, it may be that after calming the mind and deliberative thinking, they attain inner peace and harmony that is freed from deliberative thinking and attain concentration.

In the third stage, the bhikkhu remains conscious and clearly aware, and they experience happiness in their body. They attain the third absorption, and they can then think, 'I am stable in calmness'.

In the fourth stage, with the disappearance of happiness and sorrow, they enter the fourth jhana, which is beyond happiness and pain due to equanimity.

In the fifth stage, it may happen that, with the disappearance of the perceptions of the physical world and the perceptions of the senses and diversity in perceptions, they think that 'Space is infinite'. They remain in the same state of mind.

In the sixth stage of meditation, it may be that by feeling the area of the infinite space completely, they think that consciousness is infinite. Some monks enter and live in the field of infinite consciousness. In the discipline of a great person, they call it 'peaceful living'.

In the seventh stage, it may be that by freeing the area of infinite consciousness completely, someone enters and lives in the area of emptiness. At this stage, they may believe they have achieved a stable state of equanimity. In the discipline of the great person, it is called 'peaceful living.'

In the eighth stage, it may happen that, by realizing the field of emptiness, some Bhikkhus enter and live in the area of full consciousness. In the discipline of the great person, it is called 'peaceful conscious living'."

But here, Mahakund, to eliminate destruction (turbulent state of mind) and to live a peaceful, blissful and conscious-mindfulness life, you should practice the following in life ;

- Other people will be harmful, but we will not be harmful.
- Other people will kill beings, but we will be disturbed by killing beings.
- Other people will take what has not been given, but we will avoid taking what has not been given.
- Other people will be impure (impurity of mind), but we will remain pure.
- The other will lie, but we will avoid lying.
- Others will talk malicious things, but we will avoid giving malicious speeches.
- Others may speak harshly, but we will not be disturbed by their harsh speeches.

- The others may engage in gossip, but we will refrain from participating in it.
- The others may be greedy, but we will not succumb to greed.
- Others may have malicious thoughts, but we will not have thoughts of malice.
- Others' views may be wrong, but we believe our views are correct.
- The intentions of others may be wrong, but our intentions will be righteous.
- Others may use inappropriate speech, but we will strive to use the right speech.
- Others may do wrong things, but we will ensure that we do the right thing.
- Others may pursue the wrong livelihood, but we will choose the right livelihood.
- Others may make the wrong efforts, but we will ensure that our efforts are right.
- The mentality of others may be wrong, but our mindset will be correct.
- The concentration of others may be wrong, but our concentration will be correct.
- Others may have the wrong knowledge, but we will strive to have the right knowledge.
- Others may succumb to laziness and lethargy, but we will be free from such tendencies.
- Others may become excited, but we will remain unshaken and stable.
- Others may harbor doubts, but we will be free from such doubts.
- Others may become angry, but we will refrain from anger.
- Other people may be hostile, but we will not reciprocate with hostility.

- Others may try to discredit, but we will not engage in discrediting them.
- Others may be domineering, but we will not adopt a domineering approach.
- Other people may harbor malice, but we will not respond with hatred.
- Other people may be jealous, but we will refrain from feeling jealous.
- Other people may be fraudsters, but we will not deceive anyone.
- The others may be insidious, but we will not be insidious.
- Other people may be stubborn, but we will not be stubborn.
- Others may be egotistic, but we will be humble.
- Explaining it to others may be difficult, but explaining it to ourselves will be easy.
- Others may have bad friends, but we will have noble friends.
- Other people may be careless, but we will be careful.
- Others may be incredible, but we will be trustworthy.
- Others may be shameless, but we will be ashamed of our wrongdoings.
- Others may lack a conscience, but we will maintain our own conscience.
- Others may not pursue education, but we will always strive to learn new things.
- Other people may remain inactive, but we will be energetic.
- There will be a lack of awareness among others, but we will be established in awareness.
- Other people may be less intelligent, but we will be endowed with intellectual capabilities.
- Other people may misunderstand based on their personal views, and they may hold those views firmly without easily abandoning them, but we will not judge them as wrong based on our own

thoughts, nor will we hold our views firmly, but will readily abandon any incorrect perspectives.

Mahakund, who is immersed in mud itself, cannot pull out another person immersed in mud, because he is unable to get out of the mud himself. But it is possible that the person who is not immersed in the mud to take others from mud.

Mahakund, it is not possible for one who is not self-restrained, not disciplined and does not calm their desires to make others restrained and disciplined or bring them to the complete mitigation of lusts. But this is possible, Mahakund to one who is self-restrained, disciplined and has completely calmed his feelings and lusts. Such a person can help others to restrain and discipline themselves and to completely extinguish their desires.

Buddha further said to Mahakund,

"I have shown the way of liberation. I have shown the way when thoughts arise, I have given you instructions to escape, and I have shown you the way to go upwards."

"Oh, Mahakund, as a teacher, I have done what one guru is expected to do for the welfare of their students.

Mahakund, there is a tree, and there is an empty space for you. Go and meditate, Mahakund, do not delay, it is not that you have to regret later."

11. Not being attached to the concept of self

Once at Sravasti, there the Buddha made this proclamation:

"It should not be, it should not come into my mind; it will not be, it will not come into my mind. A bhikkhu established on this will break the lower fetters."

When the Buddha said this, a Bhikkhu said to the Buddha,

"How will a bhikkhu reflect on this – It should not be, it should not come into my mind; it will not be, it will not come into my mind."

The Buddha clarified this view to bhikkhus in the following manner:

"There is the case, bhikkhu, where an uneducated, ignorant person – one who has no respect for the great ones, is not well versed or disciplined in the Dhamma and he regards his physical body as 'self' or the 'self' as the form possessing it or the form as the 'self' or the 'self' as the form. He does not understand, as it really is, the non-self-form as 'non-self-form'… the non-self-feeling as 'non-self-feeling'… the non-self-perception as 'non-self-perception'… the 'non-self' creation as 'non-self' creation… the non-self-consciousness as 'not self-consciousness'.

Now, a well-trained disciple – one who has respect for the noble ones, one who has respect for the upright ones and well versed and disciplined in their Dhamma, does not regard body as the 'self" or 'self' as a body. He does not regard feeling as the 'self'… does not regard perception as the 'self'. Does not regard fabrications as the 'self'… He does not regard consciousness as the 'self'. He, as it really is, recognizes the tense feelings as a tense feeling, unstable feeling as an unstable feeling, unstable perception as an unstable perception and unstable consciousness as unstable consciousness."

The Bhikkhus then asked the Buddha, "Lord, a Bbhikkhu who understands and follows this will break the lower fetters. But, how can one know or see whether all such fetters have come to an end?"

The Buddha replied to the Bhikkhu,

"There is a case where an uneducated and ignorant person is afraid of something that is not the basis for fear. Fear is for an uneducated or ignorant person who thinks, this should not happen, this should not come into my mind, this will not happen, this will not occur to me. But a learned disciple is not afraid of any fear, as they know the cause of fear."

12. Path of Sadhamma

Members of various religious sects and people from the Brahmin community had gathered in Shravasti during one rainy season. They had invited the people of the city and organized a grand event of sermons, speeches and debates. All the learned people were given the opportunity to present the basic principles of their respective sects. Many followers of Buddha listened to this debate.

On their return, these people told the Buddha whatever they had seen and heard. They said that every possible spiritual problem was presented in this debate and during the discussion on it, every speaker tried to prove that the principles of their sect were the best. The debate started in a cordial atmosphere, but at the end, everything became a den of angry shouting and screaming.

On this, the Buddha told a story to his followers and disciples.

"Once, a clever king invited many blind people to his palace. The king called for an elephant, placed it among them and asked the blind people to describe what the elephant was like. The blind man who touched the elephant's legs said the elephant was like a pillar of a house. The blind man who touched the elephant's tail said the elephant was like a broom. The blind man who touched its ears said the elephant was like a winnowing basket. The blind man who touched its stomach said the elephant was like a round drum. The blind man who touched the elephant's head said the elephant was like an earthen pot. The blind man who touched the elephant's trunk said the elephant was like a stick.

After this, the king asked all the blind men to sit together and describe the elephant. All the blind men started discussing the elephant, although no one agreed on its true nature. No one wanted to admit they were wrong, as they had all touched and felt the elephant. There was quarreling and fighting among them. Everyone wanted to prove their views about the elephant were right."

The Buddha said to the Bhikkhus,

"Whatever the intellectuals were fighting for, their views were partial truths. What they saw and heard was only a small part of the whole truth and reality. Taking partial truth as the whole truth would result in a distorted, incomplete understanding. Similarly, a person who follows the Sadhamma correctly accepts with conviction that their knowledge is incomplete."

O Bhikkhus, to follow the Sadhamma, one needs to constantly strive to gain a deep knowledge of the Dhamma. We must make constant efforts to advance on the path of Sadhamma and study deeply, as accepting current ideas as the ultimate truth will only hinder the realization of absolute truth. The disciple must be free from all misinformation and not accept what is visible today until it has been studied and tested. Two preconditions are necessary to follow Sadhamma:

- One needs humility.
- The other is freedom of mind (mukta citta).

All the Bhikshus present expressed their gratitude to the Buddha, and after proper greetings, they all left.

13. Monks should behave decently.

Once upon a time, the Buddha lived in the Pubbarama monastery in Shravasti. Some Bhikkhus came to him complaining that some people were disturbing their Vipassana practice in various ways. After listening to all the complaints of the Bhikkhus, the Buddha asked them to listen to what he wanted to say to them.

The Buddha said,

Monks, you are advised to follow these practices.

- The person who practices Dhamma should be well behaved, well cultured, soft-spoken and of a humble nature and should not be arrogant.
- They should be contented, should not have any attachment to family, should not have many needs and should live a simple life with minimum requirements.
- They should not do such acts that can be condemned by wise people. Their mind should be filled with good wishes for every being, whether they are small or big, strong or weak, visible or invisible.
- One should not think ill of others, cheat, lie or harm anyone with malicious intent.
- They should treat all beings with the same kind of affection as a mother does to her child.

- They should always be alert, aware and live in the present moment. They should not covet and should not indulge in sensual pleasures.
- A Bhikkhu should follow the middle path. They should love even their enemies. They should demonstrate the path of Dhamma to all others.
- They should always try to conquer anger with the attitude of not being angry, conquer the wicked with goodness, conquer the miser with generosity, conquer falsehood with truth.
- Bhikkhus, try to conquer all those who are causing trouble without creating any hatred in your mind and show them the right path. Surely, they will all stop causing trouble in your practice."

After the Dhamma discussion, all the bhikkhus left after expressing their thanks to the Buddha.

After this, all the Bhikkhus started treating all the troublemakers with a very kind heart and compassion. Gradually, their troubles started to weaken.

14. Just gossiping is bad

Once when the Tathagata Buddha was residing in Jetavana, Bhikkhu Mallukyaputra came to meet him. After proper greetings, he took his place near the Buddha. He asked permission to raise some questions to the Buddha. The Buddha allowed him to ask any question.

Bhikkhu Mallukyaputra said,

"O Tathagata Buddha, whenever I start practicing Dhamma, many questions come to my mind, such as whether the world is temporary or eternal, whether the body and soul are the same or different, whether the Tathagata will be reborn after his death, and when this world was created and by whom?"

He further said, "I will accept you as my teacher only if you answer my questions."

The Buddha smiled at him and said,

"Mallukyaputra, did I ever tell you that I will answer these questions only when you become my student or did you tell me that I will become your teacher only when all the questions are answered by me."

Mallukyaputra Bhante said, "No, Lord."

The Buddha said,

"Whether you accept me as your teacher or become my student, these two are different issues. In fact, please listen carefully to what I am telling you here."

The Buddha said,

"Consider that someone is injured by a poisonous arrow and brought to a physician for treatment. If the physician says, 'Who used this arrow, was he a man or a woman, a Brahmin or a Kshatriya, rich or poor, was he black or white, what material was used to make the bow string? The physician says, 'I will not treat you unless you answer these questions.'

Mallukyaputra, unless he gets all the answers, the patient will die without treatment. Similarly, if you are determined not to practice Dhamma unless you get all the answers from me, you will die without practicing the Dhamma.

Bhante, the Buddha tells his disciples only those things that are absolutely necessary for the welfare of individuals. The Buddha never says things that have nothing to do with human happiness and welfare."

The Buddha further said,

"I treat the patient like an expert physician. You should not pay attention to things that I have never told you. Why do you want to know whether the world is permanent or impermanent, whether the soul and the body are one or separate, whether this world was created by God or some supernatural power or it came about on its own, whether there is rebirth after death or not? If we try to find answers to these questions it will be a waste of time. Such debates will not bring happiness to man."

"So, Mallukyaputra Bhante, do not ponder over things that are not relevant to human welfare. Please try to spend your valuable time in the practice of Dhamma."

Bhikkhu Mallukyaputra was satisfied with the profound explanation of the Buddha on each and every question or doubt. After proper greetings, he took leave of the Buddha.

15. Causes of all distress or annoyances

On one occasion, while in Jetavana, the Buddha addressed his disciples on the methods of overcoming all suffering and obstacles in life.

Buddha said,

"Listen and meditate on what I say. To those who see and understand to relieve all life's distress, annoyances and hindrances."

"It is a question of two things: discerning attention and undiscriminating attention.

There are some afflictions which must be overcome by discernment, by self-restraint, some by practice, by care, by patient endurance, by suppression, and others by mental exercise."

16. People invite trouble into their lives

Once in Shravasti, while addressing the Bhikkhus, the Buddha said,

"O Bhanthe, an ordinary, uneducated man who knows nothing about the great men, disrespects the learned man and is unable to distinguish between what is worthy and what is unworthy. Such persons hate the wise and learned man. He has not been taught the great principles of life, nor does he care to learn about them. Neither does he know what is worthy and what is not worthy of attention in the teachings. He does not even know what to listen and what not to listen. Such a man pays attention to things that are not worthy of attention and he pays no respect to those who are truly worthy of respect. Such persons invite trouble into their lives.

A man who contemplates on things that give rise to new thoughts of existential craving, delusion and sensual lust has struggle and suffering in life. That man does not respect those things in life that are worthy of his respect. Thus, he respects what is not worthy of respect. By not paying attention to what is worthy of attention, new conflicts and sufferings arise for him and the old conflicts and sufferings become stronger. Such thinking multiplies the suffering and unhappiness present in his life.

The wise man does not pay attention to irrelevant things or aspects. The wise man pays attention to good things, so new desires do not arise. Thus, by ignoring what is not worthy of respect and paying attention only to things worthy of respect, new sufferings do not arise from new conflicts, and those that have arisen cease."

The Bhikkhus expressed their gratitude to the Buddha and left.

17. Controlling oneself by self-restraint

The Buddha once addressed the Bhikkhus while he was in Shravasti.

"O Bhikkhus, the wise man with a controlled vision endures cold and heat, hunger and thirst, the annoyance of the wind and the bees, and all kinds of abuses. If he is unable to be patient, the curse will be severe and disastrous. Through patience and perseverance, suffering can be overcome.

O Bhikkhus, the wise person with a controlled vision overcomes uncontrolled, severe and disastrous events. The wise person controls everything in contemplation. Suffering and curses do not come near them. Through self-restraint, they overcome problems."

18. Be cautious when using food, shelter and clothes

The Buddha once addressed the Bhikkhu Sangha while he was in Shravasti.

"O Bhikkhus, the wise contemplative Bhikkhu is careful to use clothing only to the extent that it protects him from cold and heat, he uses clothing only to protect himself from bees, mosquitoes and reptiles, and only to hide his shame. The wise and contemplative man uses food only for the maintenance of his bodily functions and not for pleasure.

The wise and contemplative man is careful in using housing because it protects him from rain, sun, wind and bad weather. It provides him with the opportunity to be alone. He is very careful in using medicine in case of illness."

19. Curses that can be avoided

Once in Shravasti, the Buddha addressed the Bhikkhu Sangha.

He said,

"O Bhikkhus, the wise and contemplative man avoids furious elephants, furious horses, furious bulls, mad dogs and snakes. He avoids places where there are many tree stumps, thorns, swamps, steep slopes and cesspits. That man does not associate with or befriend the wicked, and avoids unsuitable neighborhoods. If he did not abandon them, severe and destructive curses would come upon him, whereas if he avoids these evil things, no curses come upon him. This is victory over curses through avoidance."

"O bhikkhus, the wise and contemplative person gives no room to sensual desire, ill will, malice or any other evil, harmful thoughts, but on the contrary repels them, puts them down and destroys them. If he does not suppress them, severe and harmful consequences would follow."

"O Bhikkhus, the wise and contemplative man exercises himself in that element of enlightenment called mindfulness, which arises from solitude, detachment, cessation. And with mindfulness, he develops the other six elements of knowledge - penetrating power, energy, high spirits, tranquility, concentration and equanimity (cittavritti)."

"O Bhikkhus, if now the contemplative person has overcome by discrimination those prohibitions that can be overcome by discrimination, got rid of by self-control, overcome by caution those prohibitions that can be overcome by caution, overcome by patience, such person is free from all curses. He has to bow down the desire to live, he has to break all bonds, there is a complete end to suffering by the complete end of pride."

20. The Bodhisattva is characterized by no symbols, no things.

In the *Diamond Sutra* (Vajracchedika Prajnaparamita Sutra), Subhuti, one of Buddha's chief disciples, engaged in a dialogue with the Buddha, where the nature of the Bodhisattva and the qualities of a Bodhisattva were explored.

Once the Buddha was staying in Jetavana with 1250 Bhikkhus and Bodhisattvas.

The Bhikkhus came for the Dhamma Sabha and after a while, Venerable Subhuti also came and sat down. Then Subhuti rose from his seat, put his upper robe on one shoulder, knelt on his right knee, extended his hands towards the Buddha and said,

"It is amazing, O Tathagata! "How many people have you taught, how many sons and daughters have you helped to follow the path of the Bodhisattva, how many have you helped to follow the path of Sadhamma."

After these remarks, the Buddha said to Subhuti,

"Well said, Subhuti! As you said, the Tathagata has taught how to walk the path of the Bodhisattva. Therefore, Subhuti, listen well and attentively. I will teach you what the identity of a Bodhisattva should be.

If someone says that I have chosen the vehicle of the Bodhisattva, they should think in this way."

"All the beings in this universe, whether born from an egg or born from a womb, born with form or without form, with mental faculties or without mental faculties, with perception or non-perception. As far as any conceivable form of beings is conceived, all of these should be led to perfect Nirvana. Although innumerable beings have been led to Nirvana, not really. But why not? If someone has the conception of being a Bodhisattva, such a person should generate the idea that I should lead all beings to Nirvana."

"Bodhisattvas must not think in terms of personal gain or even their own liberation. Their practice should be entirely motivated by the desire to help all sentient beings without any concern for a reward or recognition."

" One who does not have control over their thoughts and has a strong sense of 'self' cannot be called awakened. The Bodhisattva should understand that all phenomena, including the self, are empty of inherent existence. This understanding is crucial to avoid attachment and clinging to form or identity."

"Furthermore, when Bodhisattvas give gifts or donations, they do not expect appreciation. Bodhisattvas must not hold onto the idea that their virtuous actions accumulate merit. Although their actions are virtuous, they should not cling to the idea of collecting karmic rewards."

"Compassion is central to the Bodhisattva path, but this compassion is not based on conceptual thinking. It is spontaneous, free from attachment,and non-judgmental. A Bodhisattva practices compassion without focusing on ideas of who needs compassion or why."

"A Bodhisattva remains patient even in the face of difficulties and challenges. This is not just patience in the worldly sense, but an understanding that everything including suffering is empty of inherent nature."

The Buddha continued,

"What do you think, Subhuti, should the Tathagata be identified by the things they possess and by their signs?"

Subhuti replied, "I do not know."

The Tathagata Buddha said,

"Whenever signs predominate, there is error; wherever signs are absent, there is no error. So the characteristics of a Bodhisattva are no signs, no things."

The Buddha asked,

"What do you think, Subhuti, what happens by entering into the flow of Dhamma. He becomes free from any greed."

21. There is no such thing as 'soul' in this nature

Once Tathagata Buddha was staying in Jetavana. He addressed the Bhikkhus on the existence of the soul and other foolish concepts accepted by society due to its ignorance.

He said to the Bhikkhus, "Look, Bhikkhus, today I will explain about the existence of soul."

"The concept is existing in society, as propagated by some sections of society due to their selfishness, is that 'soul' is the name given to the entity which is separate from the body but exists within the body. They say that after death, the soul neither dies nor ceases to exist. The body is there to cover the soul. Some say the soul is so subtle that we cannot see it, some say it can be seen, and some say both are correct."

The Buddha further says that, "this is a foolish concept like the existence of soul. It is an obstacle to right thinking. When I say there is no soul, people call me an atheist. I denied the existence of the soul and instead proposed the theory of name-form. I propounded it after a detailed analysis of the human body. Our body is composed of two things;

- The physical body (Rupa Skandha) and
- The mental body (Nama Skandha)."

Buddha explained the concept of non-self in detail and said,

" There is no permanent, unchanging self or soul that exists within a person. Everything, including what we consider to be the 'self' is made up of constantly changing aggregates (called the *Five Aggregates* or *skandhas*):

- **Form (Rupa):** The physical body and material form.
- **Feelings (Vedana):** Sensations or experiences of pleasure, pain, and neutrality.
- **Perception (Saṃjna):** The ability to recognize and perceive objects.

- **Mental Formations (Sankhara):** Thoughts, intentions, and other mental factors.
- **Consciousness (Vijnana):** Awareness or consciousness of experiences.

"These five skadhas are working together in a flux of momentary change; they are never the same for two consecutive moments. These aggregates are impermanent and ever-changing and none of them individually or collectively constitute a permanent self. Clinging to the idea of a permanent self leads to suffering (*dukkha*), because all conditioned phenomena are transient and subject to change.

They are the component forces of the psycho-physical life. Nothing is eternal, and there is no such thing as a 'soul' in this nature. The soul cannot be found in the body, and the state of the body cannot be found in the soul. This is nothing but an illusion spread for selfish reasons. The belief in the soul or 'self' and the creator God is so strongly rooted in the minds of many ignorant people. The concept of the existence of the soul is an absurd concept."

22. Girimānanda Sutta: To Girimānanda

At one time, the Buddha was staying in Jetavan in Shravasti. A Venerable Bhikkhu Girimananda was sick, afflicted, and gravely ill. Then he went to the Blessed One. Having bowed down to him, he sat to one side.

He said to the Blessed One,

"Venerable sir, I am sick, afflicted, gravely ill. May the Blessed One teach me, may the Blessed One instruct me, out of compassion."

Buddha said, "Girimananda, you should train like this",

"You should breathe in tranquilizing the bodily processes. When you train like this, you should be clearly aware of the whole body.

You should breathe in, experiencing rapture. When you train like this, you should be clearly aware of the whole body.

You should breathe in, experiencing pleasure. When you train like this, you should be clearly aware of the whole body.

You should breathe in, experiencing the mental processes. When you train like this, you should be clearly aware of the whole body.

You should breathe in, tranquilizing the mental processes. When you train like this, you should be clearly aware of the whole body.

You should breathe in, concentrating the mind. When you train like this, you should be clearly aware of the whole body.

You should breathe in, freeing the mind. When you train like this, you should be clearly aware of your whole body.

You should breathe in while contemplating impermanence. When you train like this, you should be clearly aware of the whole body.

You should breathe in while contemplating fading away. When you train like this, you should be clearly aware of the whole body.

You should breathe in while contemplating cessation. When you train like this, you should be clearly aware of the whole body.

You should breathe in while contemplating relinquishment. When you train like this, you should be clearly aware of the whole body.

You should breathe out, concentrating the mind. When you train like this, you should be clearly aware of the whole body.

You should breathe out while contemplating relinquishment. When you train like this, you should be clearly aware of the whole body.

Then the venerable Girimananda, having delighted and rejoiced in the Blessed One's words, rose from his seat and went to his dwelling. He sat down cross-legged, keeping his body erect and maintaining mindfulness, following the instructions of the Blessed One, attended to the meditation. Soon after he did so, his affliction was alleviated.

23. Akanksha Sutta -If Bhikkhu desires

In Akankshā Sutta, Buddha begins by stating that if a monk wishes to achieve certain spiritual states or attainments, they must adhere to ethical conduct. This includes refraining from harmful actions, maintaining purity in behavior, and diligently observing the monastic precepts. Through the Akankshā Sutta, the Buddha provides a comprehensive roadmap for monks to achieve their various spiritual aspirations.

On one occasion, the Buddha was staying in Jetavana. He then addressed the monks, saying, "Monks!"

- If a monk desires to be respected and esteemed by fellow monks, he should practice virtuous conduct, restrain his senses and be devoted to the monastic rules (Vinaya).
- If a monk wishes to be free from obstacles in his practice, he should cultivate good conduct, purity in thought, speech, and action, and avoid any behavior that leads to remorse.
- If a monk desires a pure livelihood, they should avoid unwholesome ways of living and ensure that their livelihood does not cause harm to themselves or others.
- If a monk desires to lead a meaningful life, they should cultivate faith, virtue, learning, generosity and wisdom.
- If a monk wishes to develop mindfulness and clear comprehension, he should practice mindfulness in all activities and situations, maintaining awareness of the body, feelings, mind and mental objects.
- If a monk desires to achieve concentration, they should develop the four foundations of mindfulness (body, feelings, mind, and mental objects) and the four right efforts (preventing unwholesome states, abandoning unwholesome states, cultivating wholesome states, and maintaining wholesome states).
- If a monk desires knowledge and vision, they should attain concentration and then apply insight to understand the nature of phenomena, seeing them as impermanent, suffering, and non-self.
- If a monk desires liberation, they should understand and contemplate the Four Noble Truths, leading to the realization of Nibbāna.
- If a monk desires the supreme goal of the holy life (Arhatship), he should develop and perfect the Noble Eightfold Path: right view,

right intention, right speech, right action, right livelihood, right effort, right mindfulness, and right concentration."

The Blessed One said thus, and the Bhikkhus delighted in the words of the Blessed One.

24. Watthaupama Sutta

This time, the Buddha in Shravsti addressed the Bhikkus.

"Monks" - "Respected sir," they replied.

Buddha while addressing the Bhikkhu said,

"Bhikkhus, suppose a cloth is tainted and dirty and for cleaning purpose it has been immersed in some colour, whether blue or yellow or red or pink, but it will remain dirty. Why is it not clean? Because the cloth was not clean."

"Bhikkhus, suppose a cloth is clean and it has been immersed in some colour, whether it is blue or yellow or red or pink, it will take this colour but it will be clean and pure. Why is the cloth clean? Similarly, when the mind is pure, there is a pleasant, good result in the future.

And bhikkhus, what are the impurities of the mind?

- Greed and craving.
- Hatred.
- Anger.
- Hostility.
- Gossip and backbiting.
- Dominance.
- Jealousy.
- Adamant behaviour.
- Cheating.
- Procastination.
- Ego.
- Carelessness.

"O Bhikkhu, abandon them by knowing that all are impurities of the mind. When he has abandoned all impurities, he knows: I am endowed with unwavering faith in the Buddha, Dhamma and Sangha. He achieves enthusiasm for the goal. Getting benefits, enthusiasm for Dhamma, attains the pleasure associated with Dhamma. When he is happy, there is pleasure in him. When there is pleasure in the mind, his body becomes calm. When his body is calm, he feels happy. The person who is happy becomes concentrated.

Just as a dirty cloth becomes clean and shiny with the help of pure water, or just as gold becomes clean and bright with the help of a furnace. If a monk with such qualities, concentration and knowledge lives with a mind of love and compassion, he lives with a great, sublime, infinite, and free mind. The whole universe is filled with love. He remains full of compassion, sympathetic joy, and equanimity, free from enmity and malice, and with the whole universe full of equanimity.

When he knows and sees this way, his mind is freed from the cankers of sensual desire, becoming, and ignorance. When the mind is freed, knowledge becomes free, and he knows that the life of purity has been lived, the task accomplished, and nothing further remains to be done. Such a bhikkhu is called *bathed with the inner bath*."

The bhikkhus rejoiced and, with proper salutation to the Buddha, they walked away.

25. Be a successor of Dhamma.

On one occasion, the Buddha addressed the bhikkhus in Jetavana in this way:

"O bhikkhus," - "Respected Sir," they replied.

The Buddha said,

"Be a lamp unto yourselves, be a refuge unto yourselves, with no other refuge. Let the Dhamma be your lamp and your refuge. The Dhamma and Vinaya I have taught and laid down for you shall be your teacher when I am gone. Bhikkhu, be my successors in the Dhamma, not my successors in material things. If you are my successor in the

Dhamma, not my successor in material things, you will not be humiliated."

Saying this, the Buddha got up from the place and went to his place of residence.

This was a profound teaching of the Buddha for his disciples and the society at large.

26. I dwell in the fullness of emptiness

Once at the Pubbarama monastery built by Visakha in Shravasti, Bhante Ananda, getting up from his afternoon practice, went to the Buddha and, after paying his due obeisances to the Buddha, sat down on one side. He said to the Buddha:

"Tathagata, I have heard that at this moment, you dwell in the perfection of emptiness. Did I hear that correctly?"

"Yes, Ananda, you have heard, learned, studied, and understood it correctly. Before and now, I dwell in the perfection of emptiness."

"In the same way, Ananda, just as the Pubbarama monastery built by Visakha is away from the disturbance of the city: empty of the disturbance of elephants, cows, horses and donkeys; empty of the transactions of gold and silver; empty of groups of men and women, and that is all that remains to be undisturbed by that emptiness. That is, there is only the vibration emanating from the bhikkhus. In the same way, a bhikkhu, not paying attention to the disturbance of the city or to human beings, only pays attention to the vibrations emanating from the forests. He pays attention only to the perception of the forests and frees their minds. He understands that in this way, there is no disturbance from the perception of the city. In this way, there is no disturbance from the perception of human beings. In this way, there is only the disturbance that emerges from the concept of forests."

"Thus, this path is empty of the disturbances that come from the perception of the city. This path is free from the disturbances that arise from the perception of human beings. Thus, only the vibrations that come from the forest disturb the emptiness or void here."

"So that is the void that does not exist." Anand said.

"So, dear Ananda, in this case, it is the result of emptiness that gives the feeling of purity.

And then, Anand, even deeper than that, a Bhikkhu is not focusing on human activities, he is not focusing on the forests, he is not thinking about anything on the earth such as dry land or rivers or swamps, plants with branches and thorns, mountains or plains. He is only focusing on the perception of the earth. When he focuses on the earth, he is only focusing on the vibrations of the earth that come from his perception.

There is no disturbance from the perception of human beings. So, there is no disturbance from the perception of the forests. This path is free of the disturbances that arise from the perception of human beings. This path is free of the disturbances that arise from the perception of the forest. In this way, only the vibrations which emanate from the perception of the earth are disturbed."

"In this way, he regards what exists as empty. As empty, as that which does not exist; and in respect of that which remains, he understands that there is being."

"Thus, Anand, in this case, it is the result of sitting empty which transcends purity.

And again, in the next stage, it is deeper than that, it is not paying any attention to the forests, not paying any attention to the earth, he is only paying attention to the perception of the field of unlimited space. He clears his mind, frees his mind.

He understands, in this way there is no disturbance from the perception of the forests. In this way there is no disturbance from the perception of the earth. Thus, this path is empty of the disturbances emanating from the perception of the forests. This path is empty of the disturbances emanating from the perception of the earth. In this way only this is what disturbs emptiness: i.e. the vibrations which emanate from the perception—the field of unlimited space."

Anand expressed his gratitude to Buddha and left the place.

27. Be Skillful in understanding your own mind

This time the Buddha addressed the assembly of Bhikkhus in Shravsti by saying,

"If a bhikkhu is not skilled in understanding the ways of the minds of others, he may train himself in such a way that at least he will become skilled in understanding the ways of his own mind.

Bhikkhus, how does a bhikkhu become skilled in understanding the ways of their own mind?

Bhikkhus, suppose a young woman or man is in puberty and is devoted to self-beautification, and he or she wants to look at the reflection of his or her face in a clean mirror or a bowl of clean water to see if there is any dirt or dust on the face. He or she will immediately try to remove the dirt or dust. If he or she finds no dirt or dust there, he or she becomes happy inwardly and is completely satisfied and thinks, 'Oh, how beautiful I am, how good I look."

Bhikkhus, in the same way, it becomes highly instructive to examine one's own qualities in a thorough manner. A Bhikkhu should always watch their behavior. They should ask themselves the following questions:

- Do I live most of the time as a grasping person or do I live most of the time as a non-grasping person?
- Do I live most of the time as a person free from malice in the heart.
- Do I live most of the time as a person immersed in laziness, sloth, and with hatred and malice in mind?
- Do I live most of the time as a restless person or a person with a serene mind?
- Do I live most of the time as a person plagued with doubt?
- Do I live most of the time as an angry person, or do I live most of the time as a person free from anger?
- Do I live most of the time as a person free from doubt, or do I live most of the time as a person with an impure mind?

- Do I live most of the time as an enthusiastic person? Do I live most of the time as an indolent man?
- Do I live most of the time as a person without concentration in meditation or with concentration in meditation?

Bhikkhus, thus observing themselves, should arouse strong will, great diligence, enthusiasm, perseverance, undistracted passion, mindfulness, and clear understanding to overcome each of the evil and unwholesome factors. When Bhikkhus have established themselves in those excellent qualities, they should make another attempt to destroy the unwholesome qualities and reach the beyond."

The Bhikkhus expressed their gratitude to the Buddha and left.

28. Greed, hatred and delusion must be completely abandoned

Once the Buddha was staying at the Pubbarama monastery. It was a full-moon night, and all the Bhikkhus had gathered for Dhamma fellowship. Addressing the gathering, the Buddha said:

"O Bhikkhus, there are three motives that motivate voluntary action. Which three?

- Greed motivates voluntary action.
- Hatred motivates voluntary action, and
- Delusion motivates voluntary action.

Bhikkhus, whatever action is done with greed is due to greed, and the action done in the present ripens in the future.

Bhikkhus, whatever action is done with hatred is due to hatred, and the action done in the present ripens in the future.

Bhikkhus, whatever action is done with attachment is due to attachment, and the action done in the present ripens in the future.

Bhikkhus, suppose seeds that are not broken, not rotten, not damaged by wind and heat and are capable of germinating, are sown in a good field with well-prepared soil. If all the conditions for germination are ideal, these seeds will certainly germinate and grow into a huge plant.

Similarly, bhikkhus, if the action is done out of greed, motivated by greed, caused by greed, then once this greed is removed, the greed-based action also ceases, cutting off the roots to make it inactive.

Similarly, if the action is done out of hatred, arises from hatred, is motivated by hatred and caused by hatred, then once hatred is removed, the hatred-based action also ceases, cutting off the roots to make it inactive.

Bhikkhus, if the action is done from delusion, it is born from delusion, it is caused by delusion. If delusion is dispelled, the delusion-based karma is also dispelled and ceases to exist.

Bhikkhus, there are seeds that are not broken, not rotten, not damaged and are capable of germination. Suppose you were to burn these seeds in a fire and turn them into ashes. If these seeds are burned and cut off from the root, they will not be able to germinate."

The Buddha continued:

"When any action, small or large, is done by fools, born of greed, hatred, and delusion, when it has matured, it is experienced here only in this life. Therefore, the wise bhikkhu should completely abandon greed, hatred, and delusion, and attain transcendental insight and abandon all states of grief."

29. Characteristics of Foolish and Wise Persons

Once upon a time, the Buddha lived in Jetavana and he addressed the Bhikkhus.

The Buddha said to the Bhikkhus,

"Today I will describe the characteristics of foolish and wise persons." He further said, a foolish person is identified by the following characteristics.

- A fool has foolish thoughts, foolish words, and foolish actions. How does a wise man identify a foolish person? A foolish person is identified by their foolish actions, foolish words, and foolish thinking. The wise man then decides that he should not waste his time and energy in giving advice.

- Bhikkhus, if people are talking about a topical and important topic and the fool is with the crowd on the street corner, and kills living beings, steals, sexually abuses, lies, and drinks intoxicating drinks, yet he thinks that I know all the things that wise people talk about.
- Then, Bhikkhus, the fool sees that a criminal has been captured by the king and has been tortured in various ways, Bhikkhus, then the fool thinks that this robber, this wicked person has been punished for doing bad. If the king captures me, I will also receive the same punishment. This is the instance when the fool experiences unpleasantness and displeasure.
- Then, Bhikkhus, when the fool rests on a chair, on a bed, or a blanket on the floor, they think about their misdeeds of body, speech, and mind. Then the fool thinks, I did not do well. I did not fear the people who were scared. I did not turn away. I have committed evil, bloody deeds, and I will surely face their consequences. He mourns, laments, and beats his chest. Bhikkhus, this is another instance when the fool experiences unpleasantness and displeasure."

Three Characteristics of a Wise Person

"Bhikkhus, the wise man thinks for good, speaks good words, and acts wisely. The wise man experiences pleasure and happiness here and now.

- Bhikkhus, if a wise person is with a crowd on the street corner and if people are talking about some important contemporary topic, then it seems to them that people are talking about these things and they should learn these things in more detail. This is the instance when the wise man experiences pleasantness and happiness.
- Then, the wise man sees that a criminal has been caught by the king and is being tortured in various ways with canes and whips. The wise man feels that the robber or evil-doer has been punished because of their own evil actions. The wise man recognizes that the evil is not within himself, and he perceives evil as truly evil. This is the instance when the wise man experiences pleasantness and happiness.

- When the wise man rests on a chair, a bed, or a blanket on the floor, he reflects on his own good conduct in body, speech, and mind. The wise man thinks that I have not committed any sins, I have dispelled the fear of frightened people, and I have not committed any evil or bloody deeds. I have created merits, and I will reap their rewards later. He does not grieve, lament, or beat his chest, and no distractions come to mind. This is the third instance when the wise person experiences pleasantness and bliss."

30. Ananganasutta - Faults

Once upon a time, the Buddha lived in Jetavana. With the Buddha's permission, the Venerable Sariputta addressed the Bhikkhus:

"Friends, Bhikkhus," and those bhikkhus replied "Yes, friends." And the Venerable Sariputta said: "Friends, there are inferior and superior persons in the world, which are those ?"

He described inferior persons.

"Some defective persons do not know that they really have any defect. A person who is unaware of their own flaws is inferior.

A person who is without blemish but does not realize it is also inferior.

He then described superior persons.

A wise person who recognizes their own defects is superior.

The unblemished (faultless) person knows that I really have no defect. That person is superior.

When this was said, the Venerable Mahamoggallana said: Friend, Sariputta, what is the reason that of those faults, one should be inferior and the other superior?

Here, friend Mahamoggallana, this flawed person who does not know that there is actually a flaw in them will not develop an interest in it, and will not try to remove that flaw. So, they will die with a mind contaminated by greed, hatred, and delusion. Just as a bronze bowl bought from a shop or a blacksmith is covered with dust and stains, so if its owner does not clean it, they will not clean it, let it lie in the dust, and over time that bronze bowl will become even more dusty and stained. So, this flawed person who does not know that there is actually a flaw in them will not develop an interest in it and will not try to remove that flaw. So, they will die with a mind contaminated by greed, hatred, and delusion.

Friend, this flawed person who knows that there is actually a flaw in them will develop an interest in it and will try to remove that flaw. They will die with a pure mind and without greed, without hatred, and without delusion. Just like a bronze bowl bought from a shop or a blacksmith will be full of dust and stains. However, the owner will clean it. The owner never lets the bronze bowl remain full of dirt and as time passes, it will become cleaner and cleaner. In the same way, this person with a flaw, who knows that they actually have a flaw, will develop an interest and try to remove that flaw. So they will die with a pure mind and without greed, hatred, and delusion.

Friend Moggallana, this is the reason that a person having blemishes is considered inferior and the blameless person is considered superior.

Friend, the synonym of fault is anger and hatred. Friend, a fault is the wandering of thoughts, especially wandering into evil thoughts. It may be that such a Bhikkhu knows that they have fallen into a transgression. It may also be that the Bhikkhu is not aware that they have fallen into a transgression, so the Bhikkhu becomes angry and averse.

It may be that the Bhikkhu knows they have fallen into a transgression; however, the senior Bhikkhu may advise them privately, not in the midst of the community. But when that Bhikkhu is advised in the midst of the community, then the advice in the midst of the community makes that Bhikkhu angry and averse. Both anger and hatred are faults.

It may be that the Bhikkhu knows that he has fallen into a transgression. He wants a Bhikkhu to advise him, not a teacher. When it happens that a Bhikkhu is advised by a teacher instead of another Bhikkhu, he becomes angry and averse. Both anger and hatred are faults.

It may happen that a Bhikkhu wishes to be the first to ask a question and invites him to preach to other Bhikkhus, but the teacher asks a question and invites another Bhikkhu for preaching. This Bhikkhu becomes angry and turns away with hatred. Both anger and hatred are faults.

It may happen that a Bhikkhu wishes to lead the Bhikkhu while they are begging in the village. However, another Bhikkhu leads the Bhikkhu Sangha while they are begging in the village. Since another Bhikkhu leads the Bhikkhu Sangha while begging in the village, this Bhikkhu becomes angry and turns away with hatred. Both anger and hatred are faults.

It may happen that a Bhikkhu wishes to take the most prominent place in the discourse, the first bowl of water, and the first morsel of food. However, when another Bhikkhu takes the most prominent seat in discourses, the first bowl of water, and the first morsel of food, this Bhikkhu becomes angry and averse. Both anger and aversion are faults.

It may be that a Bhikkhu desires to have a chance to give thanks at the end of a meal. However, when another Bhikkhu gives thanks at the end of a meal, this Bhikkhu becomes angry and averse. Both anger and aversion are faults.

It may be that a Bhikkhu desires to teach Bhikkhu and Bhikkhuni as well as lay disciples who come to the monastery. When another bhikkhu teaches male, female, and lay disciples who come to the monastery, this bhikkhu becomes angry and averse. Both anger and aversion are faults.

It may be that a Bhikkhu desires to have the finest clothing, food, housing, and excellent facilities when he is sick. When it happens that another Bhikkhu obtains excellent robes and other facilities, this Bhikkhu becomes angry and averse. Anger and hatred are both faults.

Friends, whichever Bhikkhu is possessed of evil thoughts, whether he is a dweller in the forests, living in a hut of leaves, eating according to rules, wearing rough clothes, his colleagues do not respect and honor him.

Friends, similarly, whichever Bhikkhu is free from the wandering of evil thoughts, whether he is a dweller on the outskirts of the village, a person invited by the villagers, wearing clothes provided by householders, his colleagues respect him, because others see him, hear that he is free from the wandering of evil thoughts."

31. Asappurisa Sutta: The Virtues of an Upright and Honest Person

On one occasion, the Buddha was staying in the Jetavana, where he addressed the Bhikkhus.

He said, "Bhikkhus!"

"Yes, Lord," the Bhikkhus replied.

The Buddha said, "Bhikkhus, I will teach you the virtues of an upright person. Listen, pay attention."

"Yes, my Lords," the Bhikkhus replied.

The Buddha said:

"What is the quality of a person without integrity?"

"A person without integrity often believes they are from a high-ranking family, while viewing others as being from low-ranking families. He thinks that he is superior and because he is from a high-ranking family, he thinks highly of himself and disrespects others. This is the quality of a person without integrity.

A person without integrity may feel they are from a wealthy family, while perceiving others as being from poor families. He feels proud of his wealth and considers himself superior with extensive wealth and disrespects others. This is the quality of a person without integrity.

A person without integrity may feel that they are famous and highly respected in society. He may feel that he is famous and highly respected, but these other bhikkhus are hardly known and have little influence on others. He feels proud of this and disrespects others. This is the quality of a person without integrity.

A person lacking integrity and sincerity may feel that they receive clothing, alms, housing, and medical needs from others. He may be proud that he receives these provisions, but other bhikkhus do not receive them from disciples. He feels high and proud and disrespects other Bhikkhus. This is the quality of the insincere person.

The insincere person feels that he is a learned master of Vinaya, a Dhamma-speaker. He believes that he is a Dhamma-speaker, but these other bhikkhus are not Dhamma-speakers. He feels proud of being a Dhamma-speaker and disrespects others. This is the quality of the insincere person.

The insincere person feels that he lives alone in the forests. They may feel that they are a forest dweller, while other Bhikkhus are not. They may boast about being a forest dweller and disrespect others. This is the quality of a person without integrity.

A person without integrity may feel that they wear discarded clothes, live like a beggar, live under a tree, in a cemetery, or in the open air. They are satisfied with whatever accommodation has been assigned to them. One who eats only once a day. They may be proud that they eat only once a day, while other bhikkhus do not. They may feel proud of these practices and disrespect others. This is the quality of a person without integrity.

A person without integrity feels that they have attained the first stage of knowledge, but these other bhikkhus have not attained the same level of knowledge. He feels proud of himself for attaining the first stage of knowledge and disrespects others as a result. This behavior is characteristic of a disrespectful person.

A person without integrity or honesty feels that they have attained great Dhamma knowledge, but these other Bhikkhus have not attained it. He feels proud and disrespects others. This is the quality of a disloyal person."

Virtues of an honest man

Now, he described the virtues of an honest man. He said, "Listen, bhikkhus, the virtues of an honest person."

"An honest man feels that although he is from a high-class family, the level of greed does not end, the level of hatred does not end, the level of delusion does not end. Even though one is from a high-class family, it is still honorable and praiseworthy for him to practice Dhamma. He neither feels proud of being from a high-class family, nor considers himself superior, nor disrespects others. This is the quality of an honest man.

An honest person feels that although they are from a family of great wealth, the levels of greed, hatred, and delusion do not cease. Even though one is from a family with great wealth, when practicing and following Dhamma, he does not feel that he should be honored or praised for it. So, giving priority to the practice of Dhamma alone, he neither feels proud nor exalts himself for having a family with extensive wealth, nor disrespects others. This is the quality of an honest man or an upright person.

The honest man believes that being famous and highly respected does not eliminate the levels of greed, hatred, and delusion. Even if someone is not famous and highly respected, if he is practicing Dhamma in accordance with Dhamma, practicing skillfully, he is a person who follows Dhamma, then he should be respected for this, he should be praised for this. So, giving priority to the practice alone, he neither feels proud nor disrespects others for being famous. This is the quality of an honest person or upright individual.

The honest person feels that even though they are not receiving clothing, alms, food, shelter, and medicine or other needs, if they practice Dhamma in accordance with Dhamma, they practice skillfully. Therefore, by giving priority to practice alone, they neither exalt themselves nor degrade others for their own benefit. This is the quality of an honest person.

The honest person feels that even though he is a Dhamma-speaker and is practicing Dhamma in accordance with Dhamma, he is practicing skillfully. Therefore, giving priority to practice alone, he neither takes pride in being a Dhamma-speaker nor disrespects others. This is the quality of an honest person.

He is one who follows Dhamma. He neither feels proud of being a forest dweller nor disrespects others. This is the quality of a truthful man or honest person.

The truthful or honest person feels that eating only once a day does not eliminate the levels of greed, hatred and delusion. Though he does not eat only once a day, he is practicing Dhamma in accordance with Dhamma, practicing skillfully. He neither feels proud nor exalts himself nor disrespects others. This is the quality of a truthful man or honest person.

The truthful person feels that even after attaining the first knowledge, the second stage of knowledge, etc. he neither exalts himself in attaining knowledge nor disrespects others. This is the quality of a truthful man or honest person."

The bhikkhus were pleased with the Buddha's words.

33. Not sticking to the Dhamma teachings

Once, the Buddha was in Jetavana. The Buddha used to give Dhamma sermons to all male and female monks once every ten days. Once in Sravasti, the Buddha gave a Dhamma sermon on the topic of a joyful and happy attitude on the first day of the rainy season. Bhikkhu Arishta raised some questions about the Buddha's teachings. He himself had misunderstood the Buddha's Dhamma. Responding to the questions raised by Arishta, the Buddha told the monks that,

"Each one of you must understand the true meaning of Dhamma, if it is misunderstood, it is a problem and suffering for you and for those to whom you are going to preach it. You must listen to Dhamma teachings carefully, analyze each word carefully, and practice it carefully. Those who are skilled in catching a snake save their lives by catching the head of the snake, not the middle or the tail.

When we use our intelligence to catch a snake, similarly, we must use our intelligence while learning Dhamma. All those Dhamma teachings describe reality in nature; they are not reality itself. It is like a finger showing the location of the moon in the sky; the moon is reality, but the finger pointing to the moon is not the moon. Dhamma teachings are tools to reach the destination, like a boat taking us from this side of the river to the other side. However, the boat itself is not the bank of the river. The boat is to take us to the other side of the river; after reaching the other bank of the river, we should not take it on our head, thinking it to be treated as a wealth. Those who are wise should not take the boat with them after reaching the bank. O Bhikkhu, my

Dhamma teaching is just like a boat to take you across the problem of birth and death. Similarly, do not get attached to the Dhamma teaching because it is a means through which you achieve a happy life; the Dhamma teaching is not the ultimate goal. You should leave Dhamma teachings like a boat after attaining your goal. The Dhamma teaching is a means to reach the destination, but it is not a destination itself. All the Dhamma teachings taught by me are for achieving Nirvana (Nibbana), but do not get too attached to it."

Buddha further said,

"A blissful attitude is the real life that can be achieved while living. A blissful attitude cannot be the fulfillment of all desires, because all of them are false and disappear with time. The truth is that today's happiness can become sorrow in the future. Life should be lived naturally without holding any grudge against anyone. Being free from anger and hatred in life, and being alert to the present moment and enjoying the present moment, is the source of a blissful life. A happy and contented person enjoys the blooming flowers, innocent laughter of children, gentle breeze, clear sky, and flowing water in the river, etc. The person clearly understands the phenomena of impermanence and interdependence.

A person with a happy and blissful attitude lives life without worrying about the future and is free from all kinds of fear. They know that the flower, which is very colorful, attractive, and charming today, may wither and dry up tomorrow, so they do not feel sad when the flower dries up, but enjoy the blooming flower. They also know that one who is born will surely die one day, so they never care about death and live a blissful life without the fear of death."

The Buddha further said:

"We see many people in society living their present life in a miserable, unpleasant way in the hope of happiness in the future or in the next life. They put their lives in danger by putting their physical and mental bodies in severe pain and unpleasantness in the hope of happiness and bliss in the future or in the next life, although the real life is in the present moment. Many people believe that if they want happiness and pleasant moments in the next life, they have to undergo severe physical and mental punishment in the present moment. Some people are entangled in the present moment instead of caring about the future. This is also not good. We should not worry about the future, but should think seriously about the issues that will arise in the future and how to contemplate them. We should think contemplatively instead of worrying about the future.

We need to avoid two extremes. This kind of life is enjoyable in the present as well as in the future. To attain real joy and happiness we do not need any wealth, position, success or anything else in life except mudita, maitri, karuna and equanimity."

The bhikkhus expressed their gratitude to the Buddha and then dispersed.

34. Rules to end disputes in the Bhikkhu Sangha

Once, the Buddha was staying at Jetavana in Sravasti. Venerable Bhikkhu Mahamoggallana suggested a meeting between the senior disciples of the Buddha present at Jetavana and the monks who raised certain issues at Kosambi, so that the Buddha could prevent such conflicts from emerging in the Sangha. This meeting was chaired by Venerable Mahakashyapa.

At the beginning of the meeting, Mahakashyapa asked Aniruddha to tell the rules made by the Buddha during his stay at Veluvana, Rajagruha.

After four days of debate, seven rules were finalized which would be followed by the Bhikkhu Sangha in case of a dispute, which were named 'Saptadhikara Samata.'

Sammukha Vinaya: According to the Sammukha Vinaya rule, the disputing parties must present their views in the assembly; however, no debate or discussion should continue in order to avoid further confusion and disputed issues.

Trun Starak Vinaya: It means covering the mud with grass. The Bhikkhu Sangha will unanimously appoint a respected and revered bhikkhus to listen to the disputing parties. All the bhikkhus should feel that their words, concerns, and viewpoints will be heard by these bhikkhus. These respected Panch Bhikkhu will listen more and speak less. However, when these Panch Bhikkhu speak, their words should be for consolation, for resolving the dispute, their words should be for covering the disputed points, like covering the mud with grass. Such an attitude of the Panch Bhikkhu will help eliminate disputes, and the entire Bhikkhu Sangha will live in peace.

Smriti Vinay: In the Bhikkhus' seminar, each party has to clearly explain the disputed points with all the facts, and witnesses will be required to prove some points. Everyone will need to listen carefully to maintain peace during the meeting.

Amuda Vinaya: The Bhikkhus involved in the disputes should admit their fault, and they should give up their rigid stance on their views. Such an attitude will definitely help to calm the dispute. Negativity should be considered futile. If one of the disputing parties says that the act was done due to ignorance and an unstable mental state, and there was no intention of such a negative act, then the Sangha should consider and try to find a solution.

Tatva Bhaisya Vinay: According to this rule, the disputing bhikkhu has to admit his fault voluntarily. The Sangha needs to give more time to each party to admit their mistakes. Accepting fault is the right direction to resolve the dispute. One should not hold a grudge against each other once the dispute is over.

Yedubhuyasikiya Vinay: Bhikkhu Sangha, after hearing both the disputing parties, will give the final decision, which will be binding on both parties.

Pratigyakarak Vinay: This is the acceptance of the decision of the Bhikkhu Sangha by both the disputing parties. Once the decision is accepted, the sentence 'Gyaapti Chaturbhina Karma Vachna (ज्ञाप्ति चतुर्भिन कर्म वचन) should be recited aloud three times. Then each party accepts the final decision of the Bhikkhu Sangha and can behave accordingly.

These rules were presented to the Buddha for consideration to resolve disputes between two sects of bhikkhus. The Buddha accepted these rules for inclusion in the Sangha Vinaya.

35. Barrenness of the Mind

On one occasion, the Buddha addressed the Bhikkhu Sangh in Shravsti.

Addressing the Bhikkhu Sangha, he said,

"It is impossible for one who has not given up the five barrenness (hindrance) of the mind and has not broken the five fetters in the mind to grow and attain perfection in this Dhamma and discipline."

"What are the five mental fetters that bhikkhus have not abandoned?"

"Here, if a bhikkhu is doubtful, uncertain, undecided, and distrustful of the teacher and thus his mind does not incline toward enthusiasm, devotion, perseverance, and effort. Since their mind does not incline toward enthusiasm, devotion, perseverance, and effort to learn the Dhamma, this is the first barrenness of his mind that they have not abandoned.

Then, a bhikkhu is doubtful, uncertain, undecided, and distrustful about the Dhamma, since his mind does not incline toward enthusiasm, devotion, perseverance, and effort to learn the Dhamma, this is the second barrenness of mind that he has not abandoned.

Then, if a bhikkhu is doubtful, uncertain, undecided, and distrustful about the Sangha, and since his mind does not incline toward enthusiasm, devotion, perseverance, and effort to learn about Sangha, this is the third barrenness of his mind, which he has not abandoned.

If a bhikkhu is doubtful, uncertain, undecided, and distrustful about the training and teachings, and since their mind does not incline toward enthusiasm, devotion, perseverance, and effort to learn new things, this is the fourth barrenness of mind that they have not overcome.

Then, a bhikkhu is angry and displeased with his companions in the holy life, is wrathful and unkind to them, and thus his mind is not inclined to enthusiasm, devotion, perseverance, and effort to remove negativity in the mind, is the fifth barrenness of the heart that he has not renounced."

Buddha further said,

"Bhikkhus, anyone who has not renounced these five barrenness in the mind will not bring about growth and perfection in this Dhamma and discipline. On the other hand, any Bhikkhu who has renounced the five barrenness in his mind will bring about growth, perfection in this Dhamma and discipline."

36. Maha-Gopalaka Sutta: Sermon on the great cowherd boy

When the Buddha was staying in Jetavana, he addressed the Bhikkhus.

He said, "Listen, O Bhikkhus,"

The bhikkhus replied.

The Buddha said: "Bhikkhus, a shepherd lacks ten qualities, which is why he is unable to take care of the flock. Which ten?"

- He is not good-looking.
- He is unskilled in qualities.
- He does not protect the flock from flies and bees.
- He does not know how to dress the wounds of injured animals.
- He does not fumigate the cattle shed to prevent flies, mosquitoes, and diseases.
- He does not know the medicines to give to the animals when they are sick.
- He is not aware of the paths leading to the pastures.
- He is not skilled in tending cattle.
- He takes off excess milk from the cow's udder, causing the milk to dry up inside the udder.
- He takes no extra care of the bulls, who are the fathers and leaders of the herd.

"A herdsman who does not have these ten qualities is unable to take care for the herd."

Buddha further said that, "Similarly, any Bhikkhu who is not endowed with these ten factors is unable to achieve growth and abundance in this Dhamma-Vinaya. What are these?

- The Bhikkhu who is not skilled in understanding the reality of our body (form) does not perceive things as they truly are. Our body is composed of five great elements – earth, water, fire, air, and empty space – and the Bhikkhu does not know this. The bhikkhu lacks the skill to recognize the true nature of things.
- A fool is identified by their words, actions, and thoughts; a wise person is identified by their right actions, words, and thoughts. Thus, a Bhikkhu is unskilled in distinguishing between fools and wise people.
- The Bhikkhu lacks the skill to control harmful tendencies, just as a shepherd is unable to protect cows from bees and flies. When sensuality arises in the bhikkhu, he does not renounce, dispel, or eliminate it. The Bhikkhu accepts the arising of thoughts of ill will and harmfulness. The Bhikkhu does not abandon, remove, or erase the existence of these thoughts. The Bhikkhu accepts the arising of evil and unwholesome qualities. The Bhikkhu does not abandon, remove, destroy, or erase the existence of these qualities.
- A Bhikkhu, seeing a form with the eye, grasps objects or details, which he cannot resist greed or distress. Whether hearing a sound with the ear, smelling a scent with the nose, tasting a flavor with the tongue, perceiving a tactile sensation with the body or recognizing a thought with the mind, they grasp at objects or details, and they cannot control the faculty of the mind. Evil and unwholesome qualities like greed or distress may assail them. He does not practice with restraint. The Bhikkhu does not safeguard the faculty of the mind. The Bhikkhu cannot attain restraint regarding the faculty of the mind. Thus, a Bhikkhu does not control the senses like a shepherd does not bandage the wounds of animals.
- A bhikkhu has heard and mastered the Dhamma, but does not teach others about it in detail, nor does he try to dispel the ignorance that prevails among people, just as a shepherd does not smoke the cattle shed to drive away harmful insects. Similarly, he does not dispel the misconceptions in people's minds with his knowledge.
- The bhikkhu repeatedly visits bhikkhus who are learned, versed in the Dhamma teachings, and have memorized the Dhamma and the

Vinaya. If the Bhikkhu does not ask them questions, he does not tell them his problems. These teachers do not reveal to the bhikkhu what has not been asked, nor do they resolve their doubts about many teachings that may raise doubts. In this way, a bhikkhu does not acquire new knowledge, just as a shepherd does not look for new pastures in the forest.

- When a Bhikkhu does not know the dhamma-vinaya declared by the Tathagat, does not know the meaning, does not gain the knowledge of Dhamma, does not gain the bliss associated with Dhamma. Thus, a Bhikkhu does not know the taste of Dhamma.
- A Bhikkhu does not know the path that leads to Dhamma, just like a shepherd does not know the way to the pastures. A Bhikkhu does not understand and does not practice the noble Eight Fold path, it means he does not know the path that leads to Dhamma.
- A Bhikkhu who is not skilled in recognizing the reality in nature is like a shepherd who is not skilled in herding cattle.
- When a Bhikkhu does not show respect to the elder Bhikkhu who is senior to him, who has been ordained for a long time, and who is a fatherly figure and a leader of the community, he does not establish himself in verbal acts of goodwill or mental acts of goodwill. It is like a shepherd who does not take care of the bull in the herd, who is the leader of the herd.

A bhikkhu with these ten factors is unable to make progress in the Dhamma-Vinaya.

37. Chachakka Sutta: The Six Senses

Once the Buddha was staying in Jetavanaa. There he addressed the Bhikkhus: "Bhikkhus"

"Yes, Tathagat," the Bhikkhus replied.

"Bhikkhus, I will teach you the Dhamma that is admirable in the beginning, admirable in the middle, admirable in the end."

"As you say, Tathagata," the Bhikkhus replied.

The Buddha said,

"The six inner senses must be known. The six outer senses must be known. The six classes of consciousness must be known. The six classes of contact must be known. The six classes of feeling must be known. The six classes of craving must be known.

The six internal senses through which we experience new things are: eye-medium, ear-medium, nose-medium, tongue-medium, body-medium, and intellect-medium. These six internal mediums should be known.

The six external mediums should be known. The six external mediums are form-medium, sound-medium, smell-medium, taste-medium, touch-sensation-medium, and thought-medium. These six external mediums should be known.

The six classes of consciousness should be known. What are these?

Consciousness arises in the eye depending on the eye and form. Consciousness arises in the ear depending on the ear and sound. Consciousness arises in the nose depending on the nose and smell. Consciousness arises on the tongue depending on the tongue and taste. Consciousness arises in the body depending on the body and touch-sensation.

Consciousness arises in the intellect depending on the intellect and thoughts.

The six classes of contact should be known. What are these?

Consciousness arises in the eye depending on the eye and form, the union of the three is contact. Consciousness arises in the ear depending on the ear and sound, and the union of the three is contact. Consciousness arises in the nose depending on the nose and fragrance, and the union of the three is contact. Consciousness arises on the tongue depending on the tongue and taste, and the union of the three is contact. Consciousness arises in the body depending on the body and tactile sensations, and the union of the three is contact. Consciousness arises in the intellect depending on the intellect and thoughts, and the union of the three is contact. These six categories of contact should be known.

Six categories of feeling should be known.. what are these?

Consciousness arises in the eye depending on the eye and form, the union of the three is contact. Feeling occurs as a necessary condition with contact. Consciousness arises in the ear depending on the ear and sound, and the union of the three is contact. Feeling occurs as a necessary condition with contact. Consciousness arises in the nose, depending on the nose and fragrance; the union of the three is contact. Feeling occurs as a necessary condition with contact. Consciousness arises on the tongue, depending on the tongue and taste, and the union of the three is contact. Feeling occurs as a necessary condition with contact. Consciousness arises in the body depending on the body and tactile sensations, and the union of the three is contact. Feeling occurs as a necessary condition with contact. Consciousness arises in the intellect depending on the intellect and thoughts, and the union of the three is contact. Feeling occurs as a necessary condition with contact.

Six categories of craving should be known. What are these?

Relying on the eye and form consciousness arises on the eye, the union of the three is contact. With contact as a necessary condition, there is feeling. As feeling arises as a requisite condition, there is craving. Relying on the ear and sound consciousness arises on the ear, the union of the three is contact. With contact as a necessary condition, there is feeling. With feeling as a necessary condition, there is craving. Relying on the nose and aroma consciousness arises on the nose, the union of the three is contact. With contact as a necessary condition, there is feeling. With feeling as a necessary condition, there is craving. Relying on the tongue and taste consciousness arises on the tongue, and the union of the three is contact. With contact as a necessary condition, there is feeling. With feeling as a necessary condition, there is craving. Relying on the body and tactile sensations consciousness arises in the body, the union of the three is contact. With contact as a necessary condition, there is feeling. With feeling as a necessary condition, there is craving. Consciousness arises in the intellect depending on the intellect and thoughts, and the union of the three is contact. With contact, there is feeling as a necessary condition. With feeling there is craving as a necessary condition."

The Bhikkhu Sangha expressed gratitude to the Buddha and, after paying proper obeisance, all the Bhikkhus left.

38. Advice to Bhikkhu Punna

The Buddha was once staying in Jetavana. Then, in the late afternoon, the Venerable Bhikkhu Punna came out of retreat and went to the Buddha. After properly greeting the Buddha, he sat down on one side of the Buddha and said to him,

"Tathagata Buddha, please teach me the Dhamma briefly. Whenever I hear the Dhamma, I become solitary, quiet, diligent, ardent, and determined."

"All right then, Punna, listen and apply your mind well, I will speak."

"Yes, Tathagata " Punna replied.

The Buddha said,

"Punna, there are sights known by the eyes that are likeable, desirable, pleasing, pleasant, sensuous and arousing. If a Bhikkhu likes them, welcomes them, and is attached to them, this produces joy. When we experience pleasure, we want to repeat that joy again and again. I say that if we are attached to such joy, it is suffering.

There are sounds that are known by the ears, smells that are known by the nose, tastes that are known by the tongue, touches that are known by the body, and there are views known by the mind that are likable, desirable, acceptable, pleasant, sensual, and arousing. If a Bhikkhu likes, accepts, welcomes, and clings to them, this produces bliss. I say that attachment to bliss is suffering.

There are views known by the eyes that are likeable, desirable, pleasing, pleasant, sensual, and arousing. If a Bhikkhu does not like, accept, welcome, and cling to them, this stops further experiences, and suffering also ceases, and there are sounds that are known by the ear, smells that are known by the nose, tastes that are known by the tongue, and touches that are known by the body. There are views known by the mind that are likeable, desirable, acceptable, pleasant, sensual, and arousing. If a Bhikkhu does not like, accept, welcome, and cling to them, then he ceases further experiences of pleasant feelings. I say that the suffering also ceases."

Punna, the Buddha asked,

"Oh! Punna, after the Dhamma training is completed, where do you want to go to give Dhamma training to people"

"Tathagata, there is a country called Sunaparanta. I will stay there."

"But Punna, the people of Sunaparanta are wild, rude, and arrogant. If they abuse and insult you, what will you think of them?"

Punna said, "If they abuse and insult me, I will think, these people of Sunaparanta are kind, really kind, because they do not hit me with their fists. That is what I will think of what kind people they are."

"But if they hit you with their fists, what will you think of them then?"

Punna said, "If they hit me with their fists, I will think, these people of Sunaparanta are kind, really kind, because they do not throw stones at me."

"But if they throw stones at you, what will you think of them?"

Punna said, "If they throw stones at me, I will think, these people from Sunaparanta are kind, really kind, because they do not beat me with sticks."

"But if they beat you with sticks, what will you think of them?"

Punna said, "If they beat me with sticks, I will think, these people from Sunaparanta are kind, really kind, because they do not hit me with knives."

"But if they hit you with knives, what will you think of them?"

Punna said, "If they hit me with knives, I will think, these people from Sunaparanta are kind, really kind, because they do not take my life with sharp knives."

"But if they take your life with a sharp knife, what will you think of them?"

Punna said, "If they take my life with a sharp knife, I will think, the purpose of my life has been fulfilled because I am being killed while I am serving them, preaching the Dhamma to the people."

The Buddha said,

"Well, well Punna, you are extremely determined in your goal of preaching the Dhamma to the common man, now you can go there and I am sure you will preach the Dhamma to them fearlessly. With such self-control and calmness, you will be quite capable of staying in Sunaparanta. Now, Punna, go to Sunaparanta at your convenience."

39. Demonstration of non-conflict

The Buddha addressed the Bhikkhu Sangha while in Jetavana.

"Bhikkhus, I will teach you an explanation of non-conflict."

"Listen to what I say and listen carefully."

"Yes, Venerable Tathagata ," the bhikkhus replied.

The Buddha said this:

"One should not pursue sensual pleasure, which is low, vulgar, crude, vile, and unprofitable, and one should not pursue self-affliction, which is painful, degrading, and unprofitable. The middle path discovered by the Tathagata avoids both extremes; giving vision, giving wisdom, it leads to peace, to direct knowledge, to enlightenment, and to Nibbana. One should know what is praise and what is condemnation, and knowing both, one should neither praise nor condemn, but only teach the Dhamma. One should know how to define happiness, and know this; one should seek happiness within oneself. One should address faults privately and avoid speaking harsh, insulting words publicly. One should speak with restraint rather than hastily. One should not insist on using the local language for conversation. This is the gist of the explanation of non-conflict."

"One should not pursue sensual pleasure, which is low, vulgar, uncivilized, vile, and unprofitable; and one should not pursue self-suffering, which is painful, degrading, and unprofitable. One whose pleasure is linked to sensual desires, whose pursuit of enjoyment is low, vulgar, uncivilized, vile, and unprofitable, is a state beset by pain, annoyance, and fever, and it is the wrong way. Detachment (getting rid) from the pleasure of sensual desires is a state devoid of the vulgar, vile, pain, annoyance, frustration, and any discomfort. This is the right way of life. Detachment from self-suffering, the painful, vile, and unprofitable, is a state devoid of pain. This is the right way of life."

"The middle way discovered by the Tathagata avoids both of these extremes; giving vision, giving wisdom, it leads to peace, to direct knowledge, to enlightenment, to Nibbana. It is the Noble Eightfold Path alone, namely: right view, right intention, right speech, right action, right livelihood, right effort, right mindfulness, and right concentration. The middle path discovered by the Tathagata avoids these two extremes."

The Bhikkhu Sangha expressed their pleasure and left the place.

40. Upanisa Sutta: Supporting Conditions (Pratityasamutpada)

On one occasion, the Buddha was living in Pubbarama Monestery in Shravasti. There, the Blessed One addressed the monks as follows:

"Monks, I will teach you Dependent Origination. Listen closely, pay attention, and I will speak."

"Yes, venerable sir," those monks replied. The Blessed One said this:

"Monks, with ignorance as condition, volitional formations come to be; with volitional formations as condition, consciousness comes to be; with consciousness as condition, name-and-form come to be; with name-and-form as condition, the six sense bases come to be; with the six sense bases as condition, contact comes to be; with contact as condition, feeling comes to be; with feeling as condition, craving comes to be; with craving as condition, clinging comes to be; with clinging as condition, existence comes to be; with existence as condition, birth comes to be; with birth as condition, aging and death, sorrow, lamentation, pain, displeasure, and despair come to be. This is the origin of this entire mass of suffering, this entire chain of suffering.

"But with the remainderless fading away and cessation of ignorance comes the cessation of volitional formations; with the cessation of volitional formations, the cessation of consciousness; with the cessation of consciousness, the cessation of name-and-form; with the cessation of name-and-form, the cessation of the six sense bases; with the cessation of the six sense bases, the cessation of contact; with the cessation of contact, the cessation of feeling; with the cessation of feeling, the cessation of craving; with the cessation of craving, the cessation of clinging; with the cessation of clinging, the cessation of existence; with the cessation of existence, the cessation of birth; with the cessation of birth, aging and death, sorrow, lamentation, pain, displeasure, and despair cease. This is the cessation of this entire mass of suffering."

The Blessed One said this. The bhikkhus were delighted with the Blessed One's statement.

41. Maharahulovada Sutta: Advice to Rāhula

Once the Buddha was living in Jetavan in Shravsti. Then, the Buddha dressed and, taking his bowl and outer robe, went to the residence of the Venerable Rahula. On seeing the Blessed One (Buddha) coming, the Venerable Rahula prepared a seat and offered water for washing the feet. The Blessed One washed his feet and sat down on the seat prepared for him. Then the Venerable Rahula bowed down to him, sat down to one side, and said to him:

"Venerable Sir, how should one practice in order to gain liberation?"

The Buddha said: "Rahula, one should practice in such a way that no conceit of 'I' or 'mine' or tendencies to conceit arise in the mind."

"And how, venerable sir, should one practice in order to gain liberation?"

"What do you think, Rahula? Are the eye and other senses permanent or impermanent?"

"Impermanent, Venerable Sir."

Rahul asked again, "Venerable Sir, how should one practice in order to gain liberation?"

The Buddha said,

"Rahula, develop the meditation on loving-kindness, for when you develop the meditation on loving-kindness (maitri), any ill-will will be abandoned. Develop the meditation on compassion (karuna), for when you develop the meditation on compassion, any cruelty will be abandoned. Develop the meditation on sympathetic joy (mudita), for when you develop it, any discontent will be abandoned. Develop the meditation on equanimity (samata), for when you develop it, any aversion will be abandoned."

This sutta gives a glimpse into the Buddha's instructions to his son, Rāhula, emphasizing the impermanence of the senses and the development of loving-kindness, compassion, sympathetic joy, and equanimity as a path to liberation.

Summary

The Dhamma discourses given by the Buddha in Shravasti hold profound significance for several reasons, both historically and spiritually. Many influential figures including kings, merchants, and other prominent personalities converted to Buddhism after hearing Buddha's discourses in Shravasti. This significantly helped in spreading Buddhism. Many monastic rules and guidelines (Vinaya) for the Buddhist Sangha were established during the Buddha's time in Shravasti, shaping the structure and discipline of monastic life. The regular interaction between the monastic community and lay followers in Shravasti fostered a strong, supportive Buddhist community.

Many of the Buddha's essential teachings were delivered in Shravasti. The Dhamma discourses given by the Buddha in Shravasti are central to the understanding and practice of Buddhism. They have provided guidance, inspiration, and a spiritual foundation for countless individuals over centuries, helping to shape the spread and development of Buddhism as a major world religion. The teachings delivered in Shravasti continue to resonate with practitioners and scholars, underscoring the enduring legacy of the Buddha's wisdom.

6. VERY IMPORTANT TOURIST PLACES IN SHRAVASTI

Lord Buddha spent 45 years of his Dhamma life in the Gangetic plains of northern India, southern Nepal, and the surrounding areas. The places like Lumbini, Bodh Gaya, Sarnath, Kushinagar, Shravasti, Rajgir, Sankasa and Vaishali are important as Buddha spent some of his valuable time at these places and also gave important Dhamma discourses. Thus, these eight sites are known as the *'Eight Great Places.'*

The city of Shravasti, with its rich culture, architecture and historical essence, definitely provides a sense of inner peace. The city of Shravasti has numerous places of worship, monuments, monasteries and other sites of interest for tourists. The historical park has a captivating aura, with lush green foliage along the walls and monasteries, which is most spectacular during sunset and dawn. Monks in kasaya robes and international pilgrims, mostly dressed in white, pay homage with incense sticks and flowers at the base of the various ruined brick temples. Soft, solemn chants and the scent of incense sticks permeate in the air. The monuments are well-marked with relevant information provided by the Archaeological Survey of India.

In 1982, Thailand built a Buddhist monastery in Shravasti. In recent times, the Buddhist monastery was built as a Burmese Vihara on the initiative of Venerable Mahathero Bhante Chandramani of Kushinagar. The second one is a Chinese Buddhist monastery built by Venerable Ray Chen. There are many beautifully designed and grand Buddhist monasteries from various countries.

Once you reach Shravasti, try to visit the places associated with Buddha and other places as well. This section of the book will take you to these places and provide detailed information about them.

1. Remains of the city walls of Sravasti at Mahet site.

The walkway seen in the given picture is one of the four main city gates of ancient Shravasti, and the one closest to the Jetavana Monastery. This must have been the same road used by the Bhikkhus residing at the Jetavana Monastery during the Buddha's time, when they went to ancient Sravasti for alms (Photo from Wiki).

1. Jetavana Monastery

The Jetavana Monastery is one of the most famous Buddhist monasteries in India, attracting thousands of visitors throughout the year. It is located 2 km from the Shravasti Bus Station. The Jetavana Monastery is one of the major Buddhist monasteries in India and a top tourist destination in Shravasti. This monastery is the place where Lord Buddha spent 25 of his 45 rainy seasons (Varshavasa). Buddha preached 871 suttas, out of which 844 were preached from this very spot in Jetavana.

The main attractions are the Anand Bodhi tree, Anandakuti, Kosambkuti, and Gandhakuti, which must be visited during a trip to Jetavana Monastery.

(Author Dr.K.P.Wasnik visited Jetavan, Shravasti in Sept. 2022)

This is one of the oldest stupas, likely from the 3rd century BC, containing relics of the Buddha. A huge statue of the Buddha was also found here, which is now preserved in the Indian Museum, Calcutta.

The ancient site of Shravasti was completely forgotten until excavations began in 1863 under the guidance of Alexander Cunningham, who followed the descriptions provided by Faxian (Fa-Hien) and Hiuen Tsang in their travelogues. Sahet was the site of Jetavana Monastery, and Mahet was the present Shravasti. Most of the excavated remains at Jetavana exhibit the typical elevation and plan of early Buddhist architecture, dating back to the Kushana period with several reconstructions and renovations carried out during the Gupta period, as well as some from later periods up to the 11th-12th century AD.

When was Jetavana Vihara built?

Literary evidence shows that Tathagat Buddha spent his first rainy season in Jetavana Vihara in his 14th year of enlightenment (Bodhi). If the Buddha was born in 563 BC, then he attained Bodhi at the age of 35 years, so the year of Bodhi would be 528 BC. If he spent his first rainy season in Jetavana Vihara in his 14th year of Dhamma life, then Jetavana might have been built in 514 - 513 BC.

Who built Jetavana?

Dedicated to Gautama Buddha, Jetavana Monastery was built by Sudatta, a wealthy merchant of Shravasti, also known as Anathapindaka. When Buddha accepted the invitation of

Anathapindaka to visit Shravasti, he purchased Jetavana or Jeta Grove for the monastery from Prince Jeta, son of King Prasenjit, and gifted it to Gautam Buddha. After Veluvana in Rajgir (Rajadruha), this was the second monastery donated to Gautam Buddha by devotees.

(The sculpture of the purchase of Jetavan by Anathapindika is engraved on the Bharhut Stupa. Just below the sculpture, it is written in Dhamma script - 'Jetavana Anathapediko Deti Koti Santhaten Keta- जेतवन अनाथपेडिको देति कोटि संथतेन केता'. It means that the buyer Anathapindika offers Jetavan by spreading crores of gold coins).

In the above picture, we can see the person is standing with a pot in their hand and is making an offering of Jetavana to Anathapindika. Gold coins were brought on a bullock cart to be spread on the floor of Jetavana. The bullocks have ropes tied to their noses. The yoke has been removed from their shoulders. The cart drawn by the bullocks has moved off. A man is unloading gold coins from behind the bullock cart. The gold coins that were unloaded earlier from the cart are being spread on the floor of Jetavana by two men. The condition was that the land of Jetavana would be sold to the one who could cover it with gold coins, and Anathapindika had accepted this challenge for the Buddha.

Today, most of the ruins are the remains of temples and stupas from the Kushan period (1st - 2nd century AD). There are 3 temples here: one is a monastery with a shrine and mandapa at the center, the second is the Gandhakuti (scented chamber), and the third is the Kosambikuti, the Buddha's meditation chamber. Opposite to this, there is the stupa where the Buddha delivered Dhamma discourses. Next to it is a well where the Buddha used to bathe. Two high rectangular brick terraces marked the original promenade where the Buddha used to walk.

Gandhakuti

Gandhakuti, the residence of Gautam Buddha, was a multi-storey building made of sandalwood, which was later destroyed by fire. Gandhakuti, located in Jetavana Mahavihara, is an important place. Tathagat Buddha used to reside in it. It was named Gandhakuti due to the fragrance of sandalwood. Chinese traveler Fa-Hien, who visited in the seventh century, has also confirmed that it was a three-storey building. Now, this place is situated in the form of a temple-like stupa made of bricks. According to the description given by Fa-Hien, when Gandhakuti was originally built, it had seven sections, in which various types of offerings and decorated banners were kept, and the place was lit with lamps burning continuously. Historical documents revealed that a rat had taken the burning candle or wick of a lamp somewhere else, which caused the entire building to burn.

The original Gandhakuti was a wooden structure, but by the time the Chinese pilgrims saw it, the structure had become a two-story brick building in ruins. Only the lower walls and stone platform are now exist.

Kosambikuti

Kosambakuti was also built by Anathapindika as a meditation hall for the Buddha. Just in front of it is a long brick platform, marking the location of the original promenade used by the Buddha for walking meditation.

Anand Bodhi Tree

The Bodhi tree was planted in Jetavana at the request of Anathapindika as a symbol of worship when the Buddha left Shravasti. Ananda once asked the Buddha for permission to plant a tree in Jetavana as his followers wanted a place to offer flowers and worship when he used to go away from Shravasti. The Tathagat attained enlightenment under the Bodhi Vriksha (Peepal Tree) in Boudh Gaya, a branch of the same tree was brought and planted in Jetavana. This tree is known as Anandabodhi. Everyone wanted King Prasenjit to plant the branch, but he refused to do so. He said there is no stability in the kingdoms of kings, so it should be planted by someone who can protect it for a long time. Then Anathapindika completed this task.

When the tree grew, it is said that the Buddha blessed it by spending a night meditating under it. This ancient sacred tree still exists in its original form. It has been protected by installing iron angles and supported by bamboo. Pilgrims visiting Shravasti sit under this tree and meditate and worship by lighting lamps and candles.

Another attraction of this religious place is a large pond called Kapalpuvapbhaar, where Buddha is said to have bathed.

3. Orajhar

At a distance of 3 km from Shravasti Bus Station, Orajhar is a Buddhist site located in Shravasti, situated on the Bahraich-Balrampur Road. Orajhar is one of the popular places to visit in Shravasti.

(Author Dr.K.P.Wasnik with family visited Orajhar in Sept, 2022)

Orajhar is said to be a monastery complex situated on an abandoned hillock with a rough path covered in grass and wild bushes. In the eastern mound, excavations revealed a solid brick structure measuring 16.20 meters in diameter. At its core was a relic-vessel, which yielded bone fragments, some gold leaves, rock-crystal, silver circular laminae, and a punch-marked silver coin. The second structure was also circular, measuring 31.50 meters in diameter, built of three concentric brick walls, with the intervening space filled with earth. No intact remains were found at its core. When we reach the top of the ruins, we can see the surrounding fields. There is no pucca road for going; it is just a narrow kuccha semicircular path to reach the top.

4. Purvarama Mahavihara

A few meters from the Orajhar mound is Purvarama or Pubbarama Monastery. A narrow road leads into a secluded, semi-forested area, and a raised ground with an Ashoka Pillar is visible. Two boards describe it as a monastery built by Migara Mata Visakha. Next to the pillar is a modern room, inside which are some broken red stone relics and a Buddha statue donated by Buddhist disciples from Thailand. Many artifacts in the monastery have been destroyed due to regular thefts in the past.

(In the picture: Visakha is overseeing the construction of Pubbarama Monastery)

Visakha was a female disciple of the Buddha and a major benefactor of the Sangha. Pubbarama Monastery, which she dedicated to the Sangha with love and devotion. Apart from Jetavana, Buddha also spent some of his days and nights there at Pubbarama. He also gave many Dhamma sermons there. This place was a two-story monastery with a meditation hall and 500 residential rooms for bhikkhus on each floor. Buddha gave 23 important Dhamma sermons here. Visakha was highly respected in the Sangha for her wisdom, generosity, and managerial skills. She took charge of the Bhikkhuni Sangha and managed it efficiently. She was authorized by the Sangha to mediate in issues and disputes arising among the nuns and between the nuns and the bhikkhus.

The Chakravarti King Ashoka visited Sravasti in 232 BC and built a 20 meter long, thick pillar at this place. The Archaeological Survey of India (ASI) excavated only 2.2 meters of the pillar. It was damaged by foreign invaders between 5th century AD and the 12th centuries AD.

5. Anathapindika's Stupa - Kachi Kuti

Located 3 km from the Shravasti bus station, Anathapindika's Stupa or Kachi Kuti is an excavated monument in Shravasti. Inscriptions found on the lower part of a Bodhisattva image excavated from this site suggest that the structure dates back to the Kushana period. Chinese pilgrims Fa-Hien and Hiuen Tsang also associated this site with the stupa of Sudatta (Anathapindika). It came to be known as Kachi Kuti after a bhikkhu built a temporary temple of unbaked bricks on top of this structure.

This magnificent stupa was built by Anāthapindika, one of the Buddha's chief disciples and greatest patrons. The original name of Anāthapindika was Sudatta, an extremely wealthy man and a generous patron of the Buddha. Anāthapindika literally means 'one who feeds the helpless'. It is believed the Buddha first visited Shravasti at the invitation of Anāthapindika, whom he met in Rajagruha. The stupa is said to have been built as a shelter for Anāthapindika. The remains of the stupa consist only of a platform and steps leading to it. Despite being in ruins, this monument attracts both historians and tourists due to its magnificent carvings and architecture.

6. Angulimala Stupa - Pakki Kuti

Angulimala Stupa or Pakki Kuti is an ancient Buddhist stupa located 3 km from Shravasti Bus Station. It is one of Shravasti's famous heritage monuments and major places to visit. Angulimala Stupa is one of the important excavated structures that visitors must visit during Shravasti tour packages.

The stupa is named after the cruel bandit Angulimala from Shravasti. Angulimala was a notorious bandit who wore a garland of his victims' severed fingers. One day, the Buddha showered his friendship and compassion on him and made him his disciple. Later, Angulimala attained arhatship and established himself as one of the ideal disciples of Buddha.

Pakki Kuti or Angulimala Stupa was excavated in 1863 along with other ruins of the Shravasti city, and it is considered to be one of the largest mounds found in the Maha Kshetra of Shravasti. Both the famous Chinese travelers Fa-Hien and Hiuen Tsang mentioned this stupa in their travelogues. Based on these travelogues, Alexander Cunningham, British Archaeologist and Engineer, identified this famous tourist attraction of Shravasti as the stupa of Angulimala.

The present structure of Pakki Kuti has undergone several subsequent alterations. It appears to be a stepped structure built on a rectangular platform. Among the ruins of Angulimala Stupa, only walls, a platform, and an elevated platform with a flight of stairs can be seen. However, the structural remains of Pakki Kuti today represent construction works from different periods.

7. Ghantaghar

The World Peace Bell Park is another tourist spot located in Shravasti. Knowing the importance of this place, the government established this garden and bell in 1981. Its aim is to promote peace in the world. This place is maintained by the Horticulture Department of the Uttar Pradesh Government.

(Author Dr. K.P.Wasnik and his family members visited Ghantaghar)

Ghantaghar in Shravasti, also known as the Clock Tower, built in memory of this historical heritage. It reminds one of the ancient glory of Shravasti and its association with Buddhism. The tower is a major landmark of the city, attracting tourists and pilgrims due to its cultural and historical significance.

7. Vipassana Dhyan Kendra

At a distance of 1 km from the Shravasti bus station, Dane Mahamongkol Temple is a Buddhist temple and meditation center located in Shravasti. It is one of the popular meditation centers in India.

Dan Mahamongkol in Shravasti is the most famous and largest temple built by Buddha's disciple Maha Upasika Sithipol Bongkok of

Thailand. It is one of the two centers installed by the Upasika Sithipol Bongkot. It is the center of learning and meditation, providing an impressive experience. This center has been established with an emphasis on education to develop virtues, great knowledge, and kindness that foster peace and true happiness in the world.

For almost thirty years, the Center has been providing free training in meditation and knowledge to the public. Around 200 women from various countries are committed to promoting humanitarian service, informal education, and other charitable activities through the Center. This area offers the experience of a natural forest with freshwater reservoirs, as well as six large halls that can accommodate about 3000 guests for prayer and meditation. The center has a state-of-the-art reverse osmosis purification plant, as well as several solitary meditation huts and large dining halls.

This divine place is ideal for tourists who want to learn meditation and free themselves from stress. Visitors can learn the Vipassana Meditation method here free of charge.

9. Myanmar Math and Korean Temple

Myanmar's Buddhist and Korean temples are located in close proximity to one another. Both premises feature bells as a symbol of peace. The Korean temple's walls display numerous verses and profound quotes that serve as inspiration.

10. Shobhanath Temple

Shravasti is considered a sacred place for both Jainism and Buddhism. As mentioned above, the third Tirthankara Sambhavnath ji of Jainism was born here. Not only this, he also gave his first discourse (Divya Dhami) here.

A temple dedicated to Sambhavnath was constructed in Shravasti before the Common Era. The temple was named after the Jain Tirthankara Sambhavnath. When the Chinese Buddhist monk Fa-Hien visited Shravasti, the Sambhavnath temple was in a ruined state, with only its remnants remaining. Excavations at the site have uncovered the remnants of a new Jain temple (Shobhanath), which appears to date back to the Middle Ages. Additionally, numerous Jain statues have been found at the site.

It is believed that Sambhavnath, the third Tirthankar of Jainism, was born in Shravasti. He was born to Raja Jitari and Rani Sunsena. He sat on the throne at the age of 20, and ruled efficiently for thirty-four years, and during his reign, many reforms were brought. However, after witnessing a disappearing of black cloud, he realized the transient nature of life and renounced his throne to pursue a monastic lifestyle.

Limited excavations were conducted here in 1824-25 and 1875-76, but the details obtained from these excavations are said to be extremely brief and inconclusive.

The city's rich history is evident in its archaeological sites, ruins, and relics.

7. HOW TO REACH SHRAVASTI

Shravasti is a peaceful place. As soon as we leave Balrampur, the beauty of Shravasti begins to reveal itself just a few kilometers from the highway. Paddy fields spread far and wide, swaying in the morning air, while a busy nilgai crosses the road to graze on the fresh monsoon grass. Shravasti comes into view around the next turn, with star-rated hotels announcing its arrival.

Shravasti can be reached by road, railways, and air.

1. By Road

Shravasti 20 km from Balrampur, 30 km from Bhinga, 44 km from Gonda, 121 km from Faizabad, 155 km from Lumbini, 175 km from Lucknow, 186 km from Gorakhpur, 261 km from Kanpur, 305 km from Varanasi, 457 km from Patna, 515 km from Bodhgaya, and 537 km from Rajgir. The most convenient route to Shravasti is from Lucknow. You can easily reach Shravasti by car, as the roads are well-built, making it a convenient way to travel to the city. If you don't want to drive, you can take UPSRTC-operated state buses. These buses drop you off at the Gonda bus stand, from where you will have to take a cab or rickshaw to Shravasti. The main road running from Balrampur to Bahraich passes by the site, which can be reached via a feeder road. You can easily reach Shravasti by taking a government roadways bus that runs between Balrampur and Bahraich.

Every year, devotees from many countries, including Mongolia, Thailand, Sri Lanka, Myanmar, Korea, and Japan, visit Shravasti. Currently, the road is the primary means of reaching Shravasti. Devotees also travel to Shravasti via Bahraich from Lucknow.

2. By Air

The nearest airport to Shravasti is the Chaudhary Charan Singh International Airport in Lucknow. The airport is 188 km from the center of Shravasti city and takes approximately 4 hours to reach by public transport.

A new airport has also become operational near Shravasti. The first phase is complete and was inaugurated by the Prime Minister of India on March 10, 2024. In the second and third phases, the airport will expand to cover an area of 750 acres. Under the UDAN scheme, flights to and from Shravasti and Lucknow are now operational, and in near future, more flights to and from New Delhi Varanasi, Prayagraj and Kanpur will begin.

3. By Rail

Although the nearest railway station is Balrampur, located 17 km from Shravasti, it does not have many trains and may not be the best option. A better option could be the Gonda Junction Railway Station, located 53 km from Shravasti. Gonda Junction is a better railway station, with trains running to major cities. Gonda Junction in Uttar Pradesh is well connected to cities such as New Delhi, Mumbai, Kolkata, Agra, Lucknow, Bangalore, and Ahmedabad.

Accomodation in Shravasti

The accommodation options in Shravasti range from budget to luxury hotels, guest houses, and homestays. Visitors should book their accommodation in advance, especially during peak season and festival times, to avoid any inconvenience or disappointment. The average cost of accommodation in Shravasti ranges from Rs. 1000 to Rs. 5000 per night, depending on the type and the location. Several high-quality, star-rated hotels of international standards have been established in Shravasti over time. Hotels like Tulip Inn, Shravsti Buddha, Shravasti Residency, Sarovar, and others are located near Shravasti. Additionally, there is a well-maintained guesthouse provided by the Uttar Pradesh Tourism Development Corporation. Bookings for this guesthouse can be made through the Corporation's office in Lucknow. Some monasteries also offer accommodations.

(Dr.K.P.Wasnik (Third from Right), Author of the Book, stayed at Govt. Guest House of UP Tourism Development Corporation in Shravasti)

The Best Time to Visit Shravasti

Any time is the ideal for inner peace and spirituality, but the climatic conditions of the region also play a major role. Visiting Shravasti is comfortable during the months of October to March. The winter season is the ideal time to travel to the city and enjoy sightseeing. The summer season usually starts from April to June. It remains highly dry, and daytime temperature often reaches 45° C. In late June or early July, the monsoon season begins, bringing torrential rain and high humidity, creating difficulties for visitors.

Other Important Information

If visiting in summer, be sure to pack light clothing and a water bottle. Options for places to eat are limited. You will mostly find dhabas or some restaurants. There are several shops around Jetavana and other tourist sites where you can buy worship-related souvenirs such as Buddha's statues, prayer books, flags, and literature. The Shravasti Festival is organized every year in January, and Buddha Purnima and

Bhagwan Sambhavnath Jayanti are some other festivals that you can attend. You can follow regular discourses and teachings here. You can take photographs and record videos at all tourist destinations of Shravasti.

Why to Visit Shravasti

Shravasti, with its blend of historical grandeur, spiritual depth, and serene beauty, offers a unique and enriching travel experience. The city also provides a unique cultural experience. It hosts various religious festivals and events, attracting pilgrims and tourists from around the world. This cultural amalgamation creates a vibrant Shravasti. The tranquil environment, coupled with the historical ambiance, provides a perfect retreat for those seeking peace and introspection. The city offers various accommodation options ranging from budget to mid-range hotels, ensuring a comfortable stay for visitors. The local hospitality is warm and welcoming, enhancing the overall travel experience. The spiritual land of Shravasti acts as a hub of temples, monasteries/viharas and stupas for Buddhist and Jain pilgrims. The Holy Land with its heritage, culture, and history enchants all visitors. A journey to this peaceful yet attractive city will delight tourists and encourage them to return.

Shravasti is home to extensive ruins, including stupas, monasteries, and ancient structures dating back to the Maurya and Gupta periods, offering a glimpse into the rich history of ancient India. Whether you are a history enthusiast, a spiritual seeker, or a curious traveler, Shravasti has something to offer everyone.

8. BIBLIOGRAPHY

1. Alexander Cunningham (1871) "Ancient Geography of India", Low Price Publications, New Delhi.
2. Alexander Cunningham (1854) "Bhilsa Topes", Published by Smith Blder & Co, London.
3. Analayo, Bhikkhu *(2008)*, "The Conversion of Aṅgulimāla in the Saṃyukta-āgama", Buddhist Studies Review, *25 (2)*.
4. Bhandantcariya Buddhaghosha (1956) "The Path of Purification - Visuddhimagga", translation by Bhikkhu Nanamoli, Printed for free distribution by The Corporate Body of the Buddha Educational Foundation, Taiwan.
5. Bhikkhu Silacara (2005) "The First 50 Discourses of Gotma the Buddha," published by Aravali Books Inernational (P)Ltd., New Delhi 110020.
6. Bimala Churn Law (1935) "Memoirs of the Archaeological Survey of India - Sravasthi in Indian Literature." Published by Manager Publication, National Archives of India, New Delhi.
7. Brancaccio, Pia (1999), "Aṅgulimāla or the Taming of the Forest", East and West, 49 (1/4): 105–18, JSTOR 29757423.
8. Burlingame, Eugene Watson; Lanman, Charles Rockwell (1921) "Buddhist Legends: Introduction, synopses, translation of books 1 and 2", Harvard University Press.
9. Dhammika, Shravasti (2005) "The Buddha and His Disciples", Buddhist Publication Society.
10. Gombrich, Richard (2006) "How Buddhism Began: The Conditioned Genesis of the Early Teachings", (2nd ed.), Routledge.
11. Harvey, Peter (2013) "An introduction to Buddhism: Teachings, History and Practices (PDF) (2nd ed.)", Cambridge University Press, New York.

12. Ilchman, Warren Frederick; Katz, Stanley Nider; Queen, Edward L. (1998) "Philanthropy in the World's Traditions", Indiana University Press.
13. John, Sherab Chodzin (2009) "A Life of the Buddha", Shambhala Publications.
14. Kosuta, M. (2017) "The Aṅgulimāla-Sutta: The Power of the Fourth Kamma", Journal of International Buddhist Studies, **8** (2): 35–47
15. Kripa Shankar (1987)"Uttar Pradesh in Statistics", APH Publishing Corporation, New Delhi.
16. Law, B.C. *(1935)* "Sravasti in Indian Literature - Memoirs of the Archaeological Survey of India", Number 50, ASI.
17. Lewis, Todd (2014) "Buddhists: Understanding Buddhism Through the Lives of Practitioners", Published by John Wiley & Sons.
18. Ling, T. (1973) "The Buddha: Buddhist Civilization in India and Ceylon." Published by Temple Smith.
19. Morgan, Joyce; Walters, Conrad (2012) "Journeys on the Silk Road: A Desert Explorer", Buddha's Secret Library, and the Unearthing of the World's Oldest Printed Book. Rowman & Littlefield.
20. Radhakumud Mookherji (1928) "Ashoka", Motilal Banarsidass, New Delhi.
21. Saddhaloka (2014-06-25) "Encounters with Enlightenment", Windhorse Publications.
22. Sangharakshita (1957) "A Survey of Buddhism -Its Doctrine and Methods Through the Ages", Trirtna Granthmala, Dapoli, Pune - 411012
23. Schumann, Hans Wolfgang (2004) "The Historical Buddha: The Times, Life, and Teachings of the Founder of Buddhism", Motilal Banarsidass Publishers, New Delhi.
24. Soeng, Mu (2011) "The Diamond Sutra: Transforming the Way We Perceive the World." Published by Simon and Schuster.

25. Sudha Pai (2017) "Political Process in Uttar Pradesh: Identity, Economic Reforms, and Governance (edited)", Centre for Political Studies, Jawaharlal Nehru University, Pearson Education India.
26. Venkataramayya, M (1981) "Sravasti", Published by the Director General, Archaeological Survey of India, New Delhi.

Reports Referred:

27. Ministry of Panchayati Raj (2009) "A Note on the Backward Regions Grant Fund Programme" National Institute of Rural Development, Hyderabad.
28. District Census Handbook: Shravasti" Registrar General and Census Commissioner of India. 2011: censusindia.gov.in.
29. District Disaster Management Plan of Shravasti District 2019-20, prepared by the District Collector, Shravasti.
30. ----------(2021) "List of 121 Minority Concentration Districts.", Reserve Bank of India.

References in Hindi and Marathi (हिंदी और मराठी में संदर्भ पुस्तकें)

1. ----------(2004) "अंगुतर निकाय (भाग 1)", विपश्यना विशोधन विन्यास, इगतपुरी, महाराष्ट्र.
2. राहुल सांकृत्यायन (1952) " बुद्ध संस्कृति", सम्यक प्रकाशन, पश्चिम पुरी, नई दिल्ली.
3. ह्वेनसांग (1972) "बुद्ध की तलाश में चीनी बौद्ध यात्री ह्वेनसांग की भारत यात्रा", अनुवाद: ठाकुर प्रसाद शर्मा, सम्यक प्रकाशन, पश्चिम पुरी, नई दिल्ली.
4. राहुल सांकृत्यायन (1986) "संक्षिप्त विनय पिटक", अनुवाद: भदंत धम्मकीर्ति, भारतीय बुद्ध धम्म ज्ञान शिक्षण विद्यालय, नागपुर.
5. राहुल सांकृत्यायन (1995) "बुद्ध चर्या" सम्यक प्रकाशन, पश्चिमपुरी, नई दिल्ली.
6. राहुल सांकृत्यायन (2008) "विनय पिटक", प्रियसेन सिंह द्वारा संपादित, सम्यक प्रकाशन, नई दिल्ली.
7. धम्मानंद कोसंबी (2012) "बौद्धधर्मावरील चार निबंध", नेहा प्रकाशन, नागपूर.
8. थिक नहत हन (2016) "जह जह चरण परे गौतम के", पेंगुइन रैंडम हाउस, नई दिल्ली.
9. फाह्यान (2017) "बुद्ध की तलाश में चीनी बुद्ध यात्री फाह्यान की भारत यात्रा", अनुवाद- जगमोहन वर्मा, सम्यक प्रकाशन, पश्चिम पुरी, नई दिल्ली.

10. बौद्ध भिक्कू (2017) "सद्धर्म पुंडरिका सूत्र", सुगत बुक डिपो, नागपुर .
11. आचार्य बुद्धघोष (2019) "सुत्तनिपात अट्ठकथा (Part 1)", प्रोफेसर अंगराज चौधरी द्वारा अनुवादित, विपश्यना विशोधन विन्यास , इगतपुरी, महाराष्ट्र.
12. कौशल्यायन भदंत आनंद (2019) "बुद्ध नियमावली -भाग 1", प्रोफेसर (डॉ.) विमलकीर्ति द्वारा संपादित, बुद्धभूमि प्रकाशन, नागपुर द्वारा प्रकाशित.
13. कांबले, डी.एल. (2023) "जातक अट्ठगाथा", भदंत आनंद कौशल्यायन की कृति का मराठी में अनुवाद, धम्मसूर्य प्रकाशन, कल्याण द्वारा प्रकाशित.

Websites visited

- https://www.photodharma.net/India/Nava-Jetavana/index.htm
- www.accesstoinsight.org
- https://suttacentral.net/The middle length discourses of the Buddha (Bhikkhu Bodhi)
- https://en.wikipedia.org/wiki/Shravasti_district
- https://shravasti.nic.in/history/#:~:text=History%20of%20Shravasti%20teerth%20begins,past%20here%20after%20Bhagwan%20Adinath
- Jetavana, The Vihara . www.sacred-texts.com.
- *https://www.google.com/search?q=shambhavnath+mandir+in+shravasti+uttar+pradesh*
- https://www.oyorooms.com/travel-guide/shravasti-travel-guide/ences[edit]
- https://www.photodharma.net/India/Nava-Jetavana/index.htm
- www.accesstoinsight.org
  https://suttacentral.net/ The middle length discourses of the Buddha (Bhikkhu Bodhi)
- https://en.wikipedia.org/wiki/Shravasti_district
- https://shravasti.nic.in/history/#:~:text=History%20of%20Shravasti%20teerth%20begins,past%20here%20after%20Bhagwan%20Adinath
- SHRI SHRAVASTI TIRTH - Jain Tirthsthaans (jainknowledge.com)